If You Believe

A Memoir To Inspire Healing

Aaron Turner, Jr.

Dedication

This book is dedicated to my mother, Gloria Jean.
You taught me love, peace, and understanding. You are the best mother in the
whole wide world! I am alive because of you.
I am love because of you.

Thank you.

Acknowledgments

To my mother, Gloria, my father, Aaron Sr., and my sister, Letitia. Thank you. I Love you and I always will – in this life and in the next. We shine our light during the highest of highs and even through the family lows...you let me shine in my own way. I am forever grateful for you and our time shared.

To my nephew, Emil III, I'm so proud of you and all that you'll become. I wish you the best that life has to offer.

To my cousin Lorraine, who led prayer every night for two weeks. To Auntie Helen and my cousin Pastor Kelly—for sitting with me—crying with me—laying your hands on my chest and praying for me. Thank you.

To good friends Gerald, Kalea, Davey, Jonathan (JJ), Andre, Cari, J. Willis, Jeremy, Chris, and Stephanie—to name a few of those who stayed at my bedside for several days at a time, never losing hope... 'twas time well spent!

To the late Bob and Jeannie G. (the homeowners), who sent group prayers and blessings from churches all over Marin and Sonoma County in support of a triumphant recovery, as well as Kathy S. and family. You did everything right. Thank you.

To Jerry, Steven, and Captain Schmidt. You truly are lifesavers.

To the Santa Rosa Junior College Theatre department: Maryanne, Leslie, Laura, Theo, and Julia, and to Debbie-Ann and the SRJC

Dance department, thank you for helping me to discover movement again.

To Cindy and Richard, Larry and Koriena, Bente and Paul, and Kim Mostat, Thank you.

To my extended family, Mariah, Violet, Anthony and Susie, Laura, Craig, Liz and Sophia—Thank you all so much for loving me back!

To all those, too many to name, who helped aid in my recovery through friendship, shelter, wisdom, or prayer—and who also believed in me. Thank you. I will remember everything forever and always. There are truly too many names to mention.

To my editorial team: First of all to Dr. E. Wallace, fellow writer, editor, and friend. *If You Believe* is forever alive because of your expertise and dedication. Your steadfastness during the time of this pandemic will always impress me. Thank you so much! Secondly to Michael Ireland, my editor and friend—I cannot thank you in words. You breathed so much magic into my story. You are like an Oracle to me. I would have never finished the manuscript without you. Thirdly, to Jennifer, who helped me with the editing and designing so I could focus on the audio and video, thank you for all your invaluable input. Together we have created something that I hope will have a positive impact in the world.

Thank you all. You will always hold a special place in my heart. I mean it!

Finally, my deepest appreciation goes to my partner, my co-traveler on this journey, and the woman who shares my shell, the love of my life, Jennifer. No one can ever know how much you supported me through this journey. You are my inspiration. You are my morning, noon, and night —and I cherish every moon-phase with you. I could never love without you.

Jen has laughed with me, cried with me, and been my constant supporter and companion. Without her, this story would still be running around in my head, and she deserves many thanks for helping me to share my message.

We believe in each other, so everything is possible!

Epigraph

Let me choose my own path, to find my way,
even if it takes me through thick and thin.

You don't want me to go, but I know my destination,
And inside is where I'm going to begin...

Contents

Introducing my story

When I was a child, I learned a simple lesson that helped shape me into the adult I am today. That lesson was: "Do unto others as you would have them do unto you." It hit me hard. Those words resonated deeply. I decided at that moment to treat the world in a way that was in alignment with that simple little lesson. I truly believe that if everyone followed this one rule, the world would be a better place.

I believe in life. I believe in the afterlife. I believe in humanity. I believe in love. My goal is to inspire and uplift others, to spread love and kindness, and to be the light. I hope that after you weave through the words of my life, it will inspire you to go out into the world and do the same. May you find the light in yourself, as I have found it in myself...and may you always believe.

Thank you for reading my story. You may listen to the accompanying music by visiting: *https://ifyoubelieve.online*.

Act 1
IF YOU BELIEVE

I wake up, confused. I can't move. I'm terrified. I can't see properly—I force my left eye open and find myself in a bright white room. There's a large blue tube in my throat. Is there a hole where my voice used to be?

I realize I'm in a hospital—tubes and equipment everywhere. I'm numb from head to toe. I'm filled with fear. I'm getting flashbacks of what happened as I was driving home. There are hushed voices talking about how I hit a tree...I fade to sleep.

I wake up to the sound of loud alarms. There are doctors and nurses all around me. I'm told I've been in a coma. I experience so many emotions: fear, disbelief, frustration. I start to feel pain everywhere. I am given a shot and I quickly fall back to sleep.

Gradually, I learn that in the initial stage of my recovery; I was in a doctor-induced coma. To this day, over twenty years later, I can't recall a single moment—not from the time I passed through the green light at the intersection of Hwy 101 at Atherton Avenue to the moment I woke from the coma.

Aaron Turner, Jr.

When I woke up, in my mind I was still travelling to my destination. I remembered I was scheduled to make music that day with JJ. He didn't know I had crashed my car weeks ago, or that I had skull injuries and paralysis in both arms.

As I lay in my hospital bed, I had so many questions. What had happened in the crash? What happened to me during my "Near Death" experience?—as we commonly describe them these days. How near was I? I was told I was combative, bleeding to death, and suffocating. I heard I nearly died once in the car, was resuscitated, and later flatlined at Novato Community Hospital... and again during surgery that evening. But, I recall nothing at all from the experience—I didn't travel up a tunnel, see any bright lights, or meet any loving ancestors. I just blacked out and woke up in my body two-and-a-half weeks later. It was like a light switch turned off, then back on again. I didn't feel the pain, the needle pricks or anything at all. I wanted to know about every scar, every stitch, every pin, every titanium screw, and every surgery the doctors had performed on my body during that time. What was happening inside me? How long would it take to heal? What happened!?

I DISCOVERED THE BIBLE HAD HELPED ME—AND NOT ONLY spiritually. My grandfather, the Pastor, had taught my father, the Minister, to place a Bible under his car seat for protection. My father taught me and I took his advice to heart. That's why I had his Bible, inscribed to me ["*To my son, Aaron Matthew Turner, Jr.*"], under my driver's seat. Even though the car was a write-off, the officers looked under the seat searching (in vain) for drugs, liquor, or contraband. They found the Bible, and looked for "Aaron Matthew Turner, Sr." That's how they located my parents—and that's one reason I'm alive today.

In that hospital bed, I learned of my injuries—all of them! My face had been crushed and because of the blow-out fracture of the bones around my right eye, I would most likely never regain control of it. It would wander, and I would need to wear glasses with a special prism for that eye...perhaps forever. I was told about the injuries to various bones: there were pins in my foot, and the damage was so bad that it would take years of surgery before I could walk normally. I might never dance again. I learned that I'd had a brain hemorrhage, and while it was mild, I'd sustained brain damage that could have irreversible effects on my ability to think clearly. (I didn't know then that attending college and university would help me overcome this.)

DURING THE HOSPITALIZATION, I HAD VERY CLOSE FRIENDS BY MY side. In fact, friends and family were often at my bedside. But when they left, the hours I spent alone felt endless. I spent them thinking, reflecting, praying, planning. My father said later that he had never cried so much. My mother told me she had never prayed so much.

Me? All I wanted to do was smile...now and then. But the injuries to my face were so extreme that I might never smile again.[1]

But wait—I'm starting in the middle of my story. Let me begin at the beginning....

"The rock and the red tree" June, 2014. ...outside of my childhood window.

3

Act 2
IF YOU BELIEVE IN... FAMILY

I was born in July 1977. One of my earliest memories is sitting on a big boulder next to a large tree. When I was four years old, my parents laid the cement foundation of our new home in a small, gated community near Middletown, in Lake County, California. The tree and the boulder stood in front of the site that would become my childhood home.

Through my four-year-old eyes, that boulder was grand in every way. I could climb on top of it and stay out of harm's way. I could survey the world around me, but be within arm's length of my mother... just in case ants attacked me—killer red ants from outer, outer space. I was King, and the rock was my throne! Mounted behind my throne, growing right out of that rock, was a beautiful red tree. Green was one of my favorite colors when I was growing up, and I especially loved the green leaves of that red tree. Its leaves were round, broad, and simple, yet it was uniquely beautiful. What stood out the most about this red tree was its bark—it peeled away like chocolate shavings, then fell to the ground.

Aaron Turner, Jr.

Over long days and endless hours, I bonded with that tree. It became my fortress. It housed my Tonka trucks and the Construx of yesteryear that fueled my imagination and filled my free time.

One day, when I was playing on my rock, my mother yelled at me out of her brand-new upstairs bedroom window: "Please be careful playing around that Manzanita bush. I saw a rattlesnake on the road today. If you get bitten, you'll die, you know. And don't eat those little berries either... you'll get sick and probably die too."

Of course, what I heard was: "Mumble, mumble, something, snake... ramble, ramble, poisonous berries ... die." But one thing I heard clearly: *Manzanita*. Was she referring to my red tree? I called back: "What? What did you say, Mama?"

As she repeated herself, I interrupted. "No, I know about the snakes, Mama... but what did you call my tree?"

She called back: "Manz-za-nita! Your tree is a Manzanita bush. Don't eat the berries and watch out for poison oak trees too!"

Well, I knew about short trees and tall trees, oak trees and pine trees, old trees and young trees, but I didn't know trees could have names. I was so proud to call my red-skinned tree by its name: Mr. Manzanita. I looked at my tree in wonder. It had a name. It was my guardian and my friend.

Over the following two years, it was just me, my rock, and Mr. Manzanita ... I admired the Manzanita bush whole heartedly. It, like me, was foreign in Middletown. Little did I know how significant that tree would become about thirty years later.

———

The new home my parents were building was in Hidden Valley Lake, a small community near Middletown. It is named

Hidden Valley Lake for obvious reasons—it is a beautiful hidden lake nestled between Clear Lake and Napa Valley. For the first year or two, while they built the house, we lived in a motor home (it had a modern, 8-Track audio system!). I'd hear coyotes every night. They were far away, but I knew nothing about distance. I only knew about danger. A mountain lion or a bobcat defending their territory?... Somehow, that didn't scare me. But in the middle of the night, security guards would drive the neighborhoods (as they were mandated to do) and often, my father would jump up and rush to the windows and peek outside to check... for danger. It was strange to hear a vehicle drive up our dirt road, because there were only six houses in our neighborhood. And why not address the elephant in the room? We were the only black family in those woods.

"House by the Lake" Summer, 1984. Taken from a lookout point just above my home, overlooking Hidden Valley Lake, Ca.

Once the security vehicle had passed by, it was dark again. Like clockwork, the crickets would return, the owls would hoot, and the coyotes would cry. This was my tranquility growing up. I've never asked my sister, Letitia, whether she had the same experiences. Was she lulled to sleep by the chirping cicadas?

It took almost a year for my parents to build our home; we finished it in 1981. I was a rambunctious four-year-old who was often reminded: "Stay out of everyone's way," or "Don't get run over by that tractor," and most often: "Leave your sister alone." Letitia was almost two years older. She was learning important six-year-old things I didn't understand. I was full of imagination, luckily, because there wasn't much to do in Middletown besides pick on your sister. So, I kept myself to myself. I felt as if the world was my oyster, even in (or on) the two-by-two space of my boulder.

By the time I was turning five, I felt more independent and daring. I explored the outer reaches of the property beyond my rock. Exploring, from then on, became second nature to me. I knew nothing about city life. It was bugs and slugs, as far as the eye could see. I felt safe in nature all the time, even at a young age. My brave, but sometimes overly cautious, parents wouldn't allow me to play outside as often as I wanted, and never after dark. The house rules were strict, and I wasn't allowed to go play with friends after school. So, I played alone and imagined what other kids were doing. We had a satellite dish, so everything I learned about the outside world came from movies. Most of my habits came from the movies, good and bad. It would have been better all-around if my parents had just let me go outside, rather than let me use my wild, five-year-old imagination.

Dad worked hard, and Mom worked tandem. We had a new home in the hills, with a lake a few miles up the street. There was a private swimming pool for homeowners and their guests. It was amazing. Often, I was the first one into the pool, and always I was the last one out—every summer over twelve consecutive years, from kindergarten to grade twelve. I was blessed to have learned how to swim at five. By my teens, the diving board was my thing. Back flips, front flips, and stunt flips with friends and visitors to the lake. (Recently, in 2018, I returned to the diving board at our local recreation center pool for the first time in over twenty years. After seventeen surgeries to my foot, it amazed me I could still do back flips into the water. It felt good, remembering the good times I'd spent at the Hidden Valley Lake pool.)

"The Turner Family"

The lake and its natural surroundings were only about two miles from our house, but up and down steep hills. It was a long walk when I was young, especially at 100 degree Fahrenheit temperatures. When I was older, I rode my bike—nothing could stop me from getting to the lake. As a child (and even now when I visit), I found solitude in Hidden Valley. My fondest memories of living in Middletown are the lake and the trees.

Hidden Valley Lake is really a part of our family's heritage. I never knew my paternal grandmother, Ethel Mae, but Dad told me that when she was growing up, she spent her summers fishing on the lake with my grandfather, Joseph (whom we all called "Elder Turner"). She'd found solitude in the waves washing upon shore and the soft winds whistling through the trees—it was a peacefulness like nowhere else she'd had access to in the '60s and '70s. Hidden Valley was just that—hidden away from the Bay Area-style hustle-bustle of life in which my grandmother lived. They've owned property in Hidden Valley Lake since the '60s. They were among the first settlers in the area—even before there was an area in which to live. My Grandmother loved to fish at the lake, and my Grandfather used the peacefulness of the forest to study his bible. It's easy to find God in nature, especially at the water's edge.

My grandparents were very lucky. Ethel Mae gave birth to almost a dozen children! Each of them now have families of their own. We are a big family of faith and food: the soul and soul-food. My Grandfather was the co-founder of Bethel Temple Apostolic Church in Richmond, California: Pastor Joseph Turner. He led my father into ministry. He was kind and caring and would give the shirt off his back to anyone who needed it. Before his passing, Elder Turner blessed many souls through the church. He also left behind a legacy; the talented Turner Family Tree, book-worthy in every way—we all have musical and artistic talent. It flows through our veins. We inspire people just as he did. Isn't that what we're all here for?

2:4 *"A Key To Heaven's Gate"*

When my parents fell in love and bonded their hearts in marriage, my grandfather gifted the property in Hidden Valley Lake to them. He said, "build a house—build your church." And as I shared earlier, they did. Dad and Mom built their home from scratch in the land of Manzanita—it was beautiful, vibrant, and strong. They also helped to build the Hilltop Apostolic Church near Clearlake...in Lower Lake, Ca., where you could hear my mother belting out songs of praise every Sunday. She's been singing in church her entire life.

We are also a family full of music. My great-grandfather, King Lemuel Turner, was born and raised in Arkansas, and historically, he was a great man. Known as the inventor of the Blues in the 1920s, he was best known for Jake Bottle Blues and Way Down Yonder Blues; two of the very first 45 rpm recordings. He was also the first black Justice of the Peace in his home state and was a highly respected man.

Music comes naturally to everyone in our family. My mother sings with the range and power of a Broadway star. She's a performer but only sings in church—and lucky be the Sunday goer. My father plays guitar and likes to play Jimi Hendrix tunes to warm up, but he too only plays in church. The best show was when they'd sing and play songs like "Walk with Me, Lord" together. Priceless.

Letitia and I are both musicians—we both attended Sonoma State University (at different times) and our Liberal Arts programs included the study of music in some form or another. She plays multiple instruments and has the voice of an angel. We have ample cousins who rap, sing, and write, and uncles who play organ, drums, and bass. Music is the glue that binds us all together.

13

"My Sis Is Super Tish" June, 2014. Taken at a Fresh Choice restaurant in Santa Rosa, Ca., by Consalvo, J.

No matter which family member it is, doing every type of music, every one of us has chosen a positive message: Gospel music, Christian hip-hop, spoken word poetry... and me, the inspirational singer. My sister is making waves in Northern California. I especially love her dedication to the youth; she's always had a big heart. She started the Lime Foundation, amongst other wonderful contributions to her community, and it is clearly in our heritage to help others. I digress.

As Letitia and I got older and our home grew larger, my parents opened their doors to foster children, providing aid for special needs children. Some of the fostered children had widowed parents, others came from broken homes or were put up for adoption at birth for a host of different reasons. I was too young to understand fully or to help a lot, but I understood that being a brother and a friend helps in the development of healthy minds. That was something I could offer. To this day, I am still in contact with a handful of foster brothers and sisters, as we are brothers and sisters for life and I love them dearly. And... surprise, they come from many races. That's healing. There are children all over the world who need homes—who need love. I'm grateful to have been part of the fostering experience. I am even more grateful to have had a home.

Act 3
IF YOU BELIEVE IN... COMMUNITY

My time in Middletown was adventurous, but well contained. I refer to it as "My town in Middletime," which was the title of a motivational speech I gave to my high school at a pep rally in 2015. Middletown was aptly named: a town in the middle— between water and mountains, and between farms and cities... between despair and infinite possibility. Happily, from our property, we could see across a valley of vineyards to the gorgeous St. Helena Mountain, ten miles away. It was a magnificent monument to wake up to every morning. The lake was the main attraction of the landscape—our special Hidden Lake. Between our house and the valley was the Middletown schools and a great place to eat, growing up, called Bueller's Kitchen.

I rode the big yellow school bus for the ten-minute drive each way, to kindergarten and back home again. I especially remember those bus rides: My driver's name was Bonnie. I remember she had red hair, and she took no nonsense from disobedient passengers like me. She was so lively, vivacious, and unforgettable. She would pick us all up in the morning and we would start off by going down the big hill on Spruce Grove Road. It was a steep, forty-five-degree incline (or close to it) and I never thought the bus would make it. I was scared. Every day. I was scared to get on and rattled when I got off. But I was brave. I never wanted to be late. I believed in Bonnie and that bus made it every day.

Middletown was a community. My most memorable experiences, apart from school in those early years, were with friends—riding my bike (without a helmet) and living inside a gated community with security guards on patrol. I was safe, unlike my cousins in "the big city", where they experienced real violence.

The worst fear I had was the creepy bus ride over Spruce Grove Road hill, or a large buck crashing into our car whenever our family drove along Highway 29. It was common for drivers to hit deer—and total their cars—on that highway. I'd seen too much carnage on that road, and I hated being in a car on that highway.

MIDDLETOWN WAS A SMALL TOWN. MY SCHOOL, MINNIE CANNON Elementary, was small too. The students all grew up together, and many of us (somehow) are still in contact; we have been since our Kindergarten years. All the campuses shared the same facilities. We were K-12. Then they built the new gym, and that made all the difference; separation.

We all had one-on-one dedication from our grade school teachers, Mr. Sherill and Mrs. Pollack. For that, I'll be grateful forever. They sparked my love of learning. They taught us camaraderie and how to have fun. I can still remember all of us singing the song, "On top of spaghetti... all covered with cheese... I lost my poor meatball... when somebody sneezed." I have so many fond memories of elementary school.

One special memory is of an early field trip our first-grade class made to a place called Anderson Marsh with our teacher, Mrs. Anderson.

She taught us about arrowheads, and about how the Pomo Indians who lived in the area used quartz crystal, abalone, and their natural surroundings to live. I became obsessed with Obsidian and Quartz crystal that is gifted to the area – being surrounded by once active volcanoes; Konocti and St. Helena. Because of those field trips, I still collect them to this day. I am so grateful for these early trips where my schoolbooks came alive.

"Mrs. Anderson's Marsh". 1982. Taken in our first grade classroom alongside my first grade teacher, Mrs. J. Anderson and Kindergarten-12th grade classmate, Gerald. By Montgomery, S.

I was in the school's band from middle school on. I played clarinet and later, the alto saxophone. The late Dr. Radford (my band and choir teacher throughout all grades) held auditions for our first school musical back in eighth grade. I was nervous, but sang my heart out and I got a leading role. Mr. Radford saw a lot in me I didn't. I played alongside a classmate named Christie in the Middletown Middle School premiere of "Peace Child." I am a peaceful child. I had sung in church before, so I knew what I needed to do. I remember it like it was yesterday: my first time on stage. It was such a sweet moment. The image was powerful: black and white, boy and girl, holding hands and singing for peace. It was needed. I am proud to have been a part of that. And Christie, who passed away in 2019, was proud as well.

Christie and I sang several duets. One was titled, "I Was a Child." We sang other ensemble songs too, such as "I Want to Live" and "Mr. President." All the songs were relevant back then (and perhaps are even more relevant today). I stood in the gymnasium nervously, with a school choir, band, orchestra, and Mom and Dad and the whole town, watching and listening as we sang our first duet, to change the world for the better. We believe we did. I am still a Peace Child.

Middletown cared for its kids, because we were their beloved children. We each had our own identity. We were all little Broncos, and we grew into mighty Mustangs! My fifth-grade teacher became my principal in High School. My Physical Education Instructor, Bill Foltmer from Middle School, later became my Varsity Football Head Coach and High School P.E. teacher. Marnin Pyzer, my pee-wee baseball coach, was also my Junior-Varsity Football Head Coach. We were a small town who grew up together, young and old.

"An Angel with a Baseball Bat." *n.d Little League Baseball team photo, Coach Marnin Pyzer.*

So, I am a product of Middletown. Simple as that. I moved there at four and I left at seventeen. I grew up at Middletown Middle School, starting as a kindergartener, then a middle-schooler. Middletown was my childhood and my adolescence.

I was lucky to have a home in Hidden Valley. I watched from my rock in our front yard as our small town grew from dirt roads and wooden gates to fancy homes in a gated community with hidden cameras. Middletown grew and grew. But between September and October 2015, one of the biggest wildfires in California's history, the Valley Fire wildfire in Lake County, devastated over 70,000 acres and consumed 2,000 homes and buildings in Hidden Valley, Whispering Pines, Middletown, Cobb Mountain, and Butts Canyon Road. Our family home was one of the few groups spared—and Mr. Manzanita, my beautiful red rock, was spared too. Most families who lost their homes rebuilt. It's who you are, it's what you do in Lake County—you build resilience. If you break, you rebuild... and when you rebuild; you build stronger and better. I learned this young.

All of us Middletown kids learned resilience. We needed to... because we were risk takers. For example, in my teenage years, friends introduced me to "the Cove," a secret swimming hole. It was a death trap... a forty-to-fifty-foot jump over a cliff into deep waters... or onto rocks. Many of us jumped. I think we all survived. We were hormone-driven young men and women with very little to do, in a small town with four distinct walls that kept us trapped inside. Sometimes we took risks, and we were okay—sometimes we got in trouble. I explored, I swam, and kept as active as I could... until I could break through that fourth wall.

I DISCOVERED YOUNG LOVE IN SEVENTH GRADE. THERE WERE LOVE notes and promises of "forever"... or at least until we were ready to throw in the towel. Then, soon after falling in love, I discovered break up... and sadness, depression, and heartache. I wanted so badly to love again. I was in seventh grade, mind you.

I was a sentimental July baby. Soft and vulnerable. Quick and easy to fall in love—as expressed in the R&B style music sung by Jodeci and Blackstreet...for example. I'm referring to those late-80s / early 90s love songs. I always needed a girlfriend, or so it seemed. My guy friends were cool, but girlfriends were sweet.

I spent most of high school with my head in the clouds. I wrote poetry and long love letters. I composed songs and serenaded unsuspecting classmates... often at the worst of times. I remember singing and dedicating "Wind Beneath My Wings" by Bette Midler to my seventh-grade girlfriend, because I thought it had a sweet

21

harmony during the choruses... completely oblivious to the lyrics or meaning of the song itself. Laughingly, everyone else on the campus understood.

As a teenager, I was love-sick, always willing to do anything to fill a space in my heart. I was looking for that love I saw on TV. I felt deep emotions. And because I never experimented with drugs and didn't discover alcohol until I was out of high school, I couldn't blame my moods on stimulants. It was the Moon. I feel I was influenced by the fluctuating planetary shifts, like the

"Modeling in Maroon" *n.d. Age 16. Dawson, Sharon.*

tides, and that made me feel in-love or love-less all of the time. I guess I didn't mind. It helped me to understand love at an early age and I then pursued it, unknowingly. (Didn't we all?)

I turned my emotions into lyrics and songs. In seventh grade, I wrote and later published (in an anthology) my first poem, "For Your Eyes Only," and I've been hooked on writing ever since. In eighth grade, I was already published and my ego expanded. I began writing prose and poems for everyone—waiting to discover my next best work. I believed that "I could save the world with my words." So, why not try?

But I seldom spent my time chasing after girls who went to my school. They were like sisters and cousins. We grew up together. After first grade, I became resigned to the idea that I wouldn't marry someone from Middletown. Most of my friends at church, who were my age, were mostly my cousins. I had to dig deeper. I dreamed about that special one, beyond the gates, past the mountains, in a land far away, farther than the eye could see. Literally, I waited till summer when my family took camping trips to Thousand Trails Campground, where I was guaranteed to meet new people. Lots of people, my family included, traveled far and wide during the summers. We camped along the way. We often visited Duncans Mills Campground by the Sonoma Coastline, and another favorite was in Marysville, near Sacramento. It was always magical. Nature was magical. The trails were laced with foliage that was foreign to me, like Stinging Nettle. Luckily, there were swimming pools and streams—some leading to the infamous Bohemian Grove...so I've heard. We were kids, camping. I often met the girl of my dreams at camp... but our love would last only for the summer. At the end of the season, I returned to Middletown, still yearning for love...I was still a hopeless, July baby.

Like I said, I couldn't really meet any new girls in Middletown—even if there were any new girls in town—mostly because I didn't go out at night. There were the occasional school events like dances and rallies, or sometimes cinema nights in Clearlake. But mostly—until I graduated high school, there was no night life. We watched movies as a family. I did homework, played Super Mario, or Metroid, or Tetris to pass the time. I fiddled around on our piano, and I practiced sax in solitude. I didn't know what was going on at teenage parties... so I couldn't miss it.

Luckily, I was always surrounded by nature and could turn to music for solace. I purchased my first compact disk [CD] and discovered R & B slow jams. I purchased the album SHAI and the cassette tape Boyz II Men. I listened to the songs day and night—at least until football came along in grade eight.

In eighth grade, a group of boys in my grade that I barely knew approached me on campus: J.R. [Jeremiah] and a few other dudes. I was nervous, of course, because in childhood movies they'd create a scene like this that never ended well. A group of strangers approaching someone... and then beat-downs or fist fights would ensue...odds were not in my favour. Instead, the unforgettable change of events in my life took place just like this:

One boy approached me. "Hey, you're really fast?" he said.

Nervously, I replied, "Yes... I think so."

Another boy said, "Yeah, you are. We saw ya."

I said, "Thanks."

Then a third boy, J.R., said, "You're coming out for the team. We think you should play football." (There was a long pause.) "Do you know what that is?"

I replied, "No."

He said, "You really don't know? Here. Drop your bag, we'll show ya."

Then we all walked out to the soccer field and started throwing a football around. I wasn't good at all, but I was fast. I saw my Pee Wee baseball coach out there watching me—he would later coach me and my Junior Varsity team to a Football Championship in my freshmen year. Oh... and there were girls there too, surrounding us and cheering us along. I was interested, of course.

I said, "What is this called again?

"Football!"

And, just like Forest in the movie *Forrest Gump*, I was lucky to have been quick on that day. When each fall came around, it was football season. From eighth grade to my freshman year in college, I played football. I was a running back. I was part of a team. I loved everything about sports—I loved touchdowns, but not touching people. I never liked touching people because I was a germaphobe ... (and it wasn't until I was in my thirties that I knew I suffered, mildly, from "mysophobia" ... a treatable condition related to OCD). So, I ran—scared. Again (pseudo-quoting *Forrest Gump*) ... "Run, Turner, run!" I did just that.

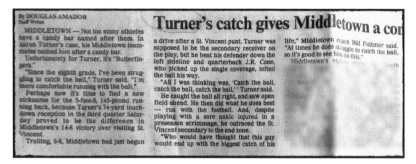

By DOUGLAS AMADOR
Staff Writer

MIDDLETOWN — Not too many athletes have a candy bar named after them. In Aaron Turner's case, his Middletown teammates named him after a candy bar.

Unfortunately for Turner, it's "Butterfingers."

"Since the eighth grade, I've been struggling to catch the ball," Turner said. "I'm more comfortable running with the ball."

Perhaps now it's time to find a new nickname for the 5-foot-6, 145-pound running back, because Turner's 74-yard touchdown reception in the third quarter Saturday proved to be the difference in Middletown's 14-8 victory over visiting St. Vincent.

Trailing, 8-6, Middletown had just begun a drive after a St. Vincent punt. Turner was supposed to be the secondary receiver on the play, but he beat his defender down the left sideline and quarterback J.R. Cone, who picked up the single coverage, lofted the ball his way.

"All I was thinking was, 'Catch the ball, catch the ball, catch the ball,'" Turner said.

He caught the ball all right, and saw open field ahead. He then did what he does best — run with the football. And, despite playing with a sore ankle injured in a preseason scrimmage, he outraced the St. Vincent secondary to the end zone.

"Who would have thought that this guy would end up with the biggest catch of his life," Middletown coach Bill Foltmer said. "At times he does struggle to catch the ball, so it's good to see him do this."

Middletown's vi...

Turner's catch gives Middletown a cor

3:5 Butterfingers...?

Since I was the second fastest kid in the entire school, my coaches liked to give me the ball. I got better and better at running faster and faster away from anyone on the field that wanted to "touch" me! I was coached so well, and I got so good at my position that I made Middletown High School Back of the Year in 1993. J.R., who recruited me in eighth grade, from then on became my quarterback and my captain, and we all contributed to a great team. We won titles for some years, and sometimes I "fumbled the ball." I experienced the highs and lows of athletics and I'd recommend it for all children, always.

3:6 "Butterfingers belies his nickname just in time", article.

Football changed me for the better. It brought a lot of the best in me, out of me, always. I had the best coaches, all of them. Although there are too many to mention, my head coaches, R. Thompson,

Aaron Turner, Jr.

Marnin Pyzer, and Bill Foltmer, stand out and have changed many lives. I scored many touchdowns running many, many yards... away from people trying to tackle/touch me. Football helped shape me into the man I am now by helping the boy I was then to discover that I had talents and skills to offer the world.

In fact, football saved me. Had it not been for football, I'd likely be in jail, dead, or living a sad lifestyle. Why? Because I'd watched television, read books, and read the newspaper. I often felt there was little hope for a young black man outside the walls of Middletown. I had a vivid imagination and was clever. In part, I was clever because I was being bullied, and I learned to retaliate—not just against the bullies, but over time, against anyone who had authority over me. Over time, I could have gotten into trouble for the lack of having nothing better to do. But football kept me busy. My mind was sound, camaraderie was epic, we were winning together (and we were losing together), as we had planned we would in eighth grade.

But outside of the good times, there were confrontations with some older students who didn't like me because I was a person of color. Specifically. The few times I was physically bullied are not significant, however, the hurtful words themselves were far worse. I internalized others' opinions and derogatory remarks towards me. I would do anything to fit in. I made a dreadful mistakes in judgment around ninth grade ,when I burglarized someones precious home. I spent the summer regretting that day. And with that experience I grew into a grade nine-and-a-halfer; smarter, tougher, and wiser . I entered tenth grade as a football star, a brave young scholar, and a leader in student-body government, prepping for college or University. What could go wrong?

ONE NIGHT WHEN I WAS SEVENTEEN, I'D BEEN OUT DANCING with a friend—the one time a year when there is an "all-county" dance held in Kelseyville, 25 minutes away. I was driving back home to Hidden Valley along California Highway 29, a dreaded two-lane highway in Middletown, in a purple VW Jetta I'd borrowed from another friend named Lisa. It was about 1:00 or 2:00 a.m. that I fell asleep at the wheel while driving back to her house. I was not drinking... I wasn't reckless... I was tired. The car veered across the margins into the oncoming traffic lane, then onto the shoulder. As the front left tires hit the gravel, I woke up sharply. In front of me was a large pine tree. I turned the steering wheel to the right immediately, over-correcting the tires, then caught traction, which shot me (at fifty miles an hour) across the two-lane road. I plummeted over a forty-foot drop. The front of the VW slammed headfirst into the ground, then hurtled back up into the air. It landed a second time on the rear passenger side and then flew back up into the air. The car landed a third (and thankfully, final) time on all four tires, facing the opposite direction, the lights still on.

I sat for a full minute inside the car. In shock. It was the middle of the night, on a highway with nothing but bucks, coyotes, crickets, a field of cattle... and most likely some snakes. I had to climb up that cliff if anyone was to know I was down there. *Was I dead? Was I broken? How much time did I have to get out of the car before it exploded?* In fact, I was safe. I wasn't harmed at all. After a minute, I got out. I crawled up to the highway and flagged down a passing car as best I could. A black kid. In the middle of the night. Nobody in Middletown knew I was there. Or so I thought.

Somehow, an ambulance arrived. I don't know who my guardian angel was that night—another driver must have seen my skid marks on the road. I was still in shock. This was my first car accident; I didn't know then that it wouldn't be my last. After the accident, I went to my Manzanita tree and my rock. That tree and that rock were still my fortress as I fought off the mood swings and trials all teenagers have to face. I'd often retreated there after fights with my parents, and this car accident was traumatic... something only my Manzanita tree and my rock could cure.

3:7 Jet Awake!

There is so much to tell about the best and worst of high school. I'd love to share more. I had a creative mind in a small town. I was eager to explore the world outside of Middletown. I wanted out! I'd have sold my soul to leave—I knew there was so much more I could offer to the world. But that outside world was inaccessible from within the gated community of Hidden Valley Lake.

Within the Hidden Valley community, I spent most of my time helping my father maintain the house, yard, and cars. I was by his side, weeding our quarter-acre lot, raking leaves in the winter, or changing the car oil in the spring. We were an average family but had a unique country home... with Mama's fried chicken and the best seafood-crab gumbo north of the south. I mean it!

Our home-life in Hidden Valley was significantly different from when we spent weekends in the Bay Area. For example, the food was noticeably different there, even though that there was an array of grocery stores to choose from. Food in the city was more processed, had more sugar, and was less healthy—that was noticeable, even for a child. I noticed a lot of fast-food lanes and little farmland. But my childhood and adolescence took place in a rural town, and I didn't have a typical west coast African-American male upbringing.

I am Congolese and Nigerian. I'm also Irish, English, and have strong Choctaw bloodlines. I was most honored to discover this with ancestry.com-styled data. While digging into my heritage, I learned that the Choctaw nation invented a game called "Little Brother of War" [or Choctaw Stick Ball] in the early 1900s which, although controversial, is known today as the national summer sport of Canada: Lacrosse. Is this why I was born to run so fast?

By the time I was in high school, I was just as much part of the Middletown community as the Pomo nation, latin and white settlers who had lived there since birth. In P.E. class, for example, there was no "black" or "white" on Coach Foltmer's court—the only race was 40 yards down the field. Jumping jacks were followed by sit-ups, pushups, and pull-ups—and another trip around the field if I complained. We were all timed, regardless of our skin color or ethnic background. We had great fitness coaches. Everybody needed to be fit and racism didn't belong in team sports.

IT'S JUNE 1995. GRADUATION DAY. I'M STANDING WITH GERALD and Raymond, Kim and Chelsea, Juanita and Bobbi, and so many other Middletown students who took the ride with me from pre-school to now. Side-by-side, the fifty-nine of us...wearing our graduation gowns, we walk down the aisle, knowing we are all feeling the same things—sad that this phase of our lives is ending, but confident that it's our turn to shift reality and make our mark on the world. I believed in my classmates.

The teachers and staff in Middletown saw that we, the class of 1995, were ready. We all had the chance to succeed – and I believe we all did; all 59 of us. We were firm and grounded like volcanic rock. Rooted like a Manzanita tree in a rock. Unstoppable ...like a California wildfire. I was eager to start my new life. I wanted to live!

As I graduated from high school and prepared to move on in life, I knew I'd have to leave my rock and my tree behind. Every day of every year as I grew up, I had stood on my rock and looked at my tree in wonder. My tree had a name. It was my guardian and my friend. It had kept me safe throughout elementary school, and had watched over me through the trials, tribulations, and triumphs of high school... and now I was saying goodbye. Where would I be without my rock and tree?

3.8 "Purple Reign"

My town in Middletime was ending. For all my years of high school, Gerald, my closest friend and I, had walked to a Deli at the other end of town, literally, for the best sandwiches around. It took us just about the entire lunch break to walk from campus to Perry's Deli. I'd order a hot Italian roast beef on dutch crunch roll with mustard, mayo, avocado, peppers, and sprouts, extra pickle, and red onions... priceless. We walked to Perry's every day we could. We'd spend the entire trip back to campus eating and talking about all the people who settled for pizza or a who knows what? I was on to something good. It was only the beginning. I was developing a palette for food.

I had cooked or watched my mother cook almost every day. She is the reason I went to culinary school. It was magic. A dash of this, a pinch of that, simmer-simmer, bang-bang, presto-change-o: "Dinner is served." It was always delicious. My father would BBQ to pitch in from time to time, but my mother is still the best chef I know. Simply magic! I had always loved food. From breakfast to lunch to dinner at home—I still do.

By the time graduation arrived, I'd already decided to become a chef. I wanted to travel the world to places like Russia and Africa (inspired by the musical, *Peace Child* and the movie, *The Color Purple*). I wanted to always eat the best food and be surrounded by people. I wanted to work on a cruise ship as a featured chef (at the time, not truly understanding the journey it would take to gain such a position).

Act 4
IF YOU BELIEVE IN... FATE

When I heard about the Culinary Arts program at Santa Rosa Junior College (SRJC), in Sonoma County, the first thing I thought of was how close to home it was—maybe too close. Still, I could leave Middletown, get away, do the adult-thing, and go to college. It was totally doable. I called and ordered a catalogue. I applied and was awarded some scholarships... most importantly, the Doyle Scholarship of $1,000 – it was truly my golden ticket.

At Santa Rosa in 1995, Culinary Arts courses cost only $11 per unit. In some semesters, my books cost more than many of my classes. I got a job at the campus bookstore and got a discount on supplies. I rented a two-bedroom apartment with my friend Gerald, another buddy, and his girlfriend.

I'd made it! I was paying rent, grocery shopping, making hard decisions, checking the locks on my front door, and navigating this chapter of my life safely and carefully. I started my new job as a server at Marie Calendars Restaurant selling pies, family meals, and singing happy birthday at least three nights a week. Culinary classes started at 6:00 a.m. every weekday and my shifts started at 6:00 p.m.

every weekend and on Friday nights. That was my last summer as an adolescent. I celebrated my eighteenth birthday that July.

I wanted a college degree in cooking more than anything else in the world, and the two worked hand-in-hand. He who controls the food, controls the world. I've heard. And he who controls his own food also controls his waistline. I know. Cooking is an art: pairing flavors from unique plants harvested from the earth, mixing ingredients, creating fondues or meringues or aioli and jams. I enjoy researching regions of food and tasting the history of each source area. I wanted to know everything about food... then, and for the rest of my life.

AT THE START OF FALL, I LEFT MY SERVING JOB TO ACCEPT A FULL-time position working for Sears in the Customer Service Office. I traded my apron for a tie. I worked there for two years—Sears was a great company to work for.

I began the full-time Santa Rosa Culinary Arts program roughly two weeks after graduation. It was the #1 Culinary Training program in the western United States and ranked third in the United States for best culinary training experience available. I completed the program in March 1998. One month after graduation, I was to head to San Francisco to complete a short course at the California Culinary Academy to prep for my entry into Princess Cruises' pilot chef program. I would have gone... except... I digress again. Let me finish talking about my love of food.

"The Culinary Artist" Oct. 1995. This photo was taken by a classmate while In attendance at Santa Rosa J.C. Culinary Arts Centre.

The Culinary Arts Program was perfect for me. It was full time and took a full three years, including summers. I moved out with Gerald, who moved on to pursue his own endeavours, and moved in with two fellow culinary students. My classmates and I formed a food-family. All three of us lived together in a three-bedroom house in Cotati, California—a university town. We worked well together in the cooking program. We literally shopped, cooked, and ate together all day, every day. Michael Salinger was the Head Chef and director of the program. He was a master chef, and I was in awe of everything he prepared. He made it look so easy. They all did. Cathy Burgett was my Baking Chef instructor and was so patient with me; she was so delicate with my learning. She was brilliant. Cathy took over the program when Michael retired. Twenty years later I still feel confident about my initial training. I've never failed a dinner party in my adult life.

I learned about Charcuterie and Garde Manger. I learned how to pronounce both correctly, and then execute them for a grade. We began with knife skills, safety and sanitation, food-borne illness, and the sciences of cooking. I was in heaven. Not only was I succeeding in the program, I was successfully filling my stomach with so much rich gourmet food—I knew I'd made the right decision about preparing to become a chef.

Aaron Turner, Jr.

I ALSO LOOKED FORWARD TO FOOTBALL PRACTICE AND ATTENDING dance classes. Yes, that was my mix. Football, food, and fancy footwork. But football only lasted the summer into the fall semester —I broke my finger first day out....and I was puny in comparison to other players. So, I "gave up" football, and it was easy to commit to a full-time cooking program with dance on the side after that. I couldn't afford knives, cleats and tap shoes anyway.

Ballet was a prerequisite to modern jazz, and (later) hip-hop dance classes at the SRJC. Only a week into ballet class I was stripped of my remaining pride—I was 5'6" and 180+ lbs. I couldn't do first, second, or third position, let alone the fouettés and jetés I would need later to progress. I was too buff for ballet. Clearly, I was a singer who liked to cook. I would not be a football star... and I had no plans to dance on Broadway! I had hopes of completing the culinary program in three years, and maintaining a secure job while I pursued a singing career. I wanted to sing more than just the national anthem for my college's football game. To feed my performance bug, I looked to join a band.

COLLEGE WAS NOT JUST ABOUT THE FOOD FOR ME. NOT AT ALL. Around February 1996, during my freshman year, I competed in the first Amateur Night Talent Contest hosted by Sway, a DJ from 106.1 KMEL (a popular Bay area radio station). It was being held at the brand-new Evert B. Person Theater at Sonoma State University.

It was a packed house. I was nervous, of course, but confident that the gospel song I was singing a capella, written by a favourite band, The Winans, would bring the crowd to their feet. It did not. They laughed at me for my choice of attire. I was wearing black slacks, church shoes, and a fancy silver show shirt that sparkled. Over that, I wore a transparent grey rain coat. Partway through my performance, the men in the crowd booed. But the women started cheering me on, and then they stood up. So, I sang louder and more confidently, for the ladies supporting me... so they screamed louder... and then the judges blew my time whistle, to my relief.

This was a Hip-Hop and R&B radio station, but on a wine country campus. I understand why there was such a mixed audience. The others competing, the judge, the DJ, and those who paid to see the show were die-hard Hip Hop fans. I didn't have a chance. I remember every act. There were two local heroes, both great rappers, competing obviously. There were two singers from Novato, a large Christian Hip Hop group that covered the entire stage (they should have won), and several other acts, too many to mention. It was good times and good music. I came in "fourth place." I was the best loser that night.

At the end of the event, I started networking with the winners immediately. They up'd my game, immediately, and thank goodness —I was behind the times. Over the next few months we all produced some songs together. I sang background vocals for some of their projects, and programmed keyboards on others—they rapped for my songs or helped with beats. The two singers from Novato were Jonathan Jones Jr. (JJ) and David Casper. I had already been singing with Andre Williams, Jr., a close friend I'd met in 1994 when we were both chosen to sing in the Lake County Honor Choir. Andre is a fantastic singer. I'd lost contact with him after I graduated from High School. It was 1996 and JJ, Casper, Dre, and I, Junior, combined our voices to form a boy-band called "Pleasure Point." We spent the next couple of years performing in and around the San Fransisco bay area. We are all still in contact now. Also, the Hip-Hop Gospel group and I recorded and released several songs on two albums, but sadly, we've lost touch over the years. And the list goes on. [1]

Aaron Turner, Jr.

4:3, 4:4 "Pleasure Point hits the proverbial 'G'-spot", 1996

Pleasure Point hits the proverbial 'G'-spot

Arielle Kohn

R&B group Pleasure Point showed students their raw talent at noon in the quad on Friday, Oct. 24. Aaron "Junior" Turner, 20; David Casper, 18; Jonathan "JJ" Jones, 19; and Andre Williams, 19, make up the group, whose music comes straight from the heart.

Pleasure Point sings in four-part harmonies, and the members take turns singing tenor or bass. The group's music is all original.

Pleasure Point was founded 5 months ago, and is currently recording a demo. The members are all self-taught musicians. Just listening and learning from other artists on the radio has been enough to teach and inspire them to want to put out their own songs.

The group defines their music as R&B, but in a more traditional sense of the word. Inspired by groups such as "The Temptations," they want to bring the "love" back into the music.

All of the songs performed were romantic in nature. The lyrics didn't refer to sex or taking your clothes off. They reflected upon happiness and love. Group member Casper did perform one song towards the end of their set that was a little bit heated, but the girls in the crowd loved it.

Students in the quad responded well to the music. To see four guys up there with only a microphone and a backup tape to sing to was impressive. The keyboard was introduced into some of the songs by Turner, who is the only member of the group attending SRJC. This is Turner's fifth semester, and he is a culinary arts major.

Pleasure Point performed some cover songs as well. Their interpretation of the old song "Still of the Night" was done beautifully.

The variety of music performed in the quad has improved greatly. It seems like a breath of fresh air whenever someone gets up there and does something that isn't the norm.

When groups like Pleasure Point perform, all types of people listen – even those that normally wouldn't listen to R&B. Student Renee Simpson stated that she usually listens to rock, but she liked their music – especially their voices.

Pleasure Point will be singing at the Phoenix Theatre on Nov. 28. The show starts at 9 p.m. and is titled "Junee Juice."

I believed in the choices I was making. I was a chef by day and a singer by night. I was living the dream! I was learning along the way. At college, I became a new man. No longer the boy who sat alone on the rock, I soon became a leader. Just as I had done at the end of my senior year when I was President of the Interact Club and ASB interim Vice-President, I encouraged my culinary friends to persevere through the pitfalls that face so many students. People who saw the joy in life as I do surrounded me.

Aside from my successes in cooking and in music, or the mega-success from my job at Sears, there was a grander lesson yet to be learned. I would be tested. The '90s were trial-and-error. All that I knew, all that I had learned until that point, would soon come to fruition. My father had told me, "Get a profession. A craft. Find a service and use it to make money." He wanted me to learn a trade. I had agreed, but I also wanted the entire college experience. I'll never look back and say that I made the wrong decision. I balanced work and education during the day, and reserved the nights for karaoke at Acapulco's Mexican Restaurant or the Flamingo Hotel. It was all a part of my journey. All of it.

IT WAS MARCH 1998. I HAD COMPLETED MY LAST EXAM FOR THE culinary program. I was a Culinary Artist and ready to show the world my perfectly developing palette. I purchased a new set of knives... I was down-sizing my life and preparing for graduation. It was time to move on from Santa Rosa. I was bound for San Francisco, come hell or high-water (as my mother would say)... I had only one more month to earn my Associate's degree. In three years, I'd grown from cooking fried Spam sandwiches on a freshman's budget to making fresh seafood paella on the fly.

I was living my dream life—cooking, studying, auditioning, and performing. I performed at schools, churches, and clubs in Santa Rosa. I spent more time with groups of singers than I did with my own friends and family. They were all my family. With a tour of concerts, studio appearances, and auditions, I was getting a little burned out, and I hadn't even begun yet. I'd heard you have to move to L.A. to make it—and I was planning to move to San Francisco to continue my chef studies at the California Culinary Academy that summer. Did life have other plans for me?

Aaron Turner, Jr.

This photo was taken by a fellow student during a teen leadership conference/camp in Westminster Woods, California. 1993. This is the only photo taken of me doing a backflip. I love it! The photographer was aspiring to be a professional - unfortunately I do not know his name.

I WAS FINISHING UP MY LAST MONTH IN THE SRJC CULINARY ARTS Program and was slated for graduation in May. A friend of mine, Erin, was going to her prom with friends and her boyfriend was deployed in the military, so she didn't have an escort. I was honored to be her date. She was 18 and I was 20. It was a fun and non-romantic event— it was better than my own prom night experience.

I had another set of friends who graduated that year and they were having a party out at Bodega Bay, along the California coastline. They invited me to join them. Since my evening with Erin was complete, I said yes, and drove twenty-five miles along the coast to a party already in progress. And instead of wasting time reliving details of a beach house party I was barely present for—I'd rather share other events taking place in my life.

I was homeless at the time. Yes, I was homeless. I'd ended the lease on my apartment and was living out of my car—just till graduation from SRJC. A family friend was kind enough to take me in for a few weeks—in exchange, I cooked and helped around their very, large home (it seemed to me to be a mansion). He lived in Bahia, California—between Novato and Benicia. They were kind to me. I came and went as I pleased, and it was a wonderful blessing during this transition between colleges. I only had another month to go.

Back in Bodega Bay, no one was expecting me anywhere. I had no curfew and nothing scheduled. I hung out at the beach with friends for a while, and when they returned to the house to party, I didn't see a reason not to stay at the beach all night. I was alone often, sitting and enjoying the tranquility of Salmon Creek Beach near Bodega. After a bit, I walked up to the house, checked in with everyone, and made sure they all had a safe ride home. I felt good about doing my part. Then I went back down to the beach. At sun rise I hiked back up the long trail of steps from the beach to the parking lot. I shook off the sand and packed my car for the journey. I realized I was tired. I was yawning and wishing I had left sooner. I knew I had to drive slowly on the way back to keep myself safe—I was on my way.

Act 5
IF YOU BELIEVE IN... GOD

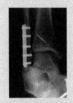

April 26, 1998. I'd finally left the ocean side in the early morning, between 6:00 and 8:00 a.m. I got into my burgundy 1989 Honda Accord to make the hour-long trip from the beach house back to Bahia. I hadn't slept at all, but thought nothing of it. I'd just cleared the off-ramp at Atherton Avenue in Novato. I turned left onto Atherton, traveling east to Bahia and drove through a green light. I was less than five miles from the home I was staying at. That green light is the last thing I remember. Within seconds of crossing the green-lit intersection over Hwy 101 at Atherton Avenue, my eyes closed as I drifted down a small grade.

I learned later that I'd gained speed to over 40 mph, but somehow, even after my car had approached a turn... I'd stayed in my driving lane. I'd slammed head-on into an oak tree, just outside a sleeping couple's bedroom window. I was told that my car burst into smoke and flames immediately—with me trapped inside, combating for my life.

The car caught fire but didn't explode. A resident of the home next door to the site of the wreckage, Jeanie Ground, told me that a pair of couples came out of their homes to discover a black man dying in a smoking car, but they didn't know what to do next. Fearlessly, Jeanie's husband, Bob, began hosing down the car hoping it wouldn't explode. Others ran inside to call 911. Although paramedics were dispatched, it could have taken them five to fifteen minutes to reach my location and then it would have taken even more time for the extraction, because Bahia was at the farthest north-eastern tip of Novato, which meant that the hospital was across town. I was close to a residential area just off the highway. An off-duty paramedic, who was driving home from his overnight shift, heard the call on his CB radio, and immediately responded to save my life.

"1989 Honda Accordion". *April, 1998. Photograph taken by the California Highway Patrol {archives}.*

My Honda Accord was an "Accordion," only recognizable as an actual vehicle from the rear end. I can say the same about my-self—my face, my skull, my body, and right foot were all unrecognizable. It took two jaws of life working simultaneously to get me out, partly because I was wearing my seatbelt. It was an absolute miracle that I didn't fall asleep at the wheel until after I got off the off-ramp. Luckily I slammed into someone's home who was able to respond. Bob tackled the smoking, flaming car bravely. Terrified and anxious, the neighbors stood nearby and watched as the paramedic worked steadfastly on my body. I was bleeding heavily. My face was crushed and planted firmly into the steering wheel. The car was still smoking and ready to burst into flame at any second. It did not.

"The Collision and the Aftermath" *from the Jaws of Life. April, 1998.*

The paramedic told me I was taking a lot of blood into my lungs. I wasn't breathing—I was choking ... drowning in my own blood. I wouldn't have been able to make the trip to the hospital, he said. There wasn't enough time. He told me later that he'd talked to me as he worked. "You're taking in a lot of blood," he'd said, as he made a small incision in my throat and inserted a temporary tracheotomy tube into my lungs to open an air passage. He drained the blood from my lungs and resuscitated me. I breathed again.

Literally, he saved my life. I was rescued from a situation that, within minutes, would have led to my absolute death; not just near death. There would not have been enough time. I learned later from Dr. Levin that, between impact and stabilizing my body after surgery, I

Aaron Turner, Jr.

had been dead for a total of four to five minutes. I overheard it as 45 minutes, and immediately began to share it with the world. Until I was corrected. I will always remember that a homeowner, who could have been a victim, and an off-duty paramedic who was not obligated, both saved my life. There are a lot of forces at work here, and it locks me firm in my belief in God, Angels, and my Spirit Guardian. For this and many reasons—I am blessed!

Moments later, several other paramedics and members of the Novato Police Department arrived to assist me. Using two jaws of life simultaneously, they removed my limp body from the crushed and mutilated Honda and eased me onto a stretcher. They needed to sedate me heavily many times (so I've been told), as I was in an extremely combative state. "You were fighting for your life, Aaron," one paramedic (and a classmate at SRJC), Erin, explained when I thanked her years later for caring for me.

The paramedics, officers, including the late Captain Steve Rucker, who was also the head of the rescue team, Captain Schmidt, who was the jaws of life operator (also the strongest man in the world), and the neighbors all cheered as they removed me from the car and placed me in the ambulance. But as the ambulance pulled away, no one really thought that I'd survive. It would take a miracle. I heard later that Jeannie had set up prayer groups in their community, praying for my recovery.

I would not have survived without them.

> y severe traumatic brain injury in a single car mot
> seatbelted driver on 4/26/98. He was rendered t
> illy taken to Nevada Community Hospital where
> ferred to Marin General Hospital. He was se
> mities. Toxicology screen was negative. CT
> etechial hemorrhages bifrontally and in the left te
> emorrhagic involvement in the brain stem on t

Medical Report. "Toxicology Screen was Negative" April/May, 1998. I felt it was important to include this here, so there is no doubt in your mind that I was not under the influence while driving. (Error: 'Nevada' is Novato)

And I did survive. I was wearing a seat belt. I wasn't drunk—I wasn't driving recklessly—I fell asleep at the wheel. The officers who investigated the scene were able to identify me by the dedication in the Bible I kept under the driver's seat. As I mentioned earlier, keeping that Bible, there was a lesson in faith my dad had bestowed upon me. It bears repeating that the inscription read: "Dedicated to my son, Aaron Matthew Turner, Jr", because that's part of the complete miracle of my survival. The officers noticed the "Jr" and located my father, Aaron Matthew Turner, Sr, and made contact. My parents gave them my medical information, and because of that, I am here to write this story.

[Unknown/CHP] "Jaws of Life" April 26, 1998. Two Jaws of Life were working, in tandem, to extract my body—and to save my life.

My family was two hours away when they got the call. I was in the ICU. My new and extremely harsh reality was unfolding before my eye... singular... as I only had one good eye.

When word of my accident got out, it spread like wildfire in Middletown and in the Bay Area. The LOVE rained down from both my Grandfather's church in Richmond and my Cousins' church in Berkeley, the Covenant Worship! But my friends and mentors in my college town, Santa Rosa, didn't know about my accident until much later. The communities were about one hour apart, and what happened in Novato wasn't news in Santa Rosa.

Depressingly, a vigil was set up at the accident site. I was told that everyone was hoping in their heart of hearts that I'd survived, but based on what they'd seen and experienced, they prepared for bad news. Someone inscribed on the tree: "In Loving Memory of Aaron Turner, April 27, 1998."

"In Loving Memory of Aaron Turner"—April 27, 1998. This photo was taken a year later.

They rushed me to Novato Community Hospital. The hospital was about eleven minutes away from the scene of the accident. Given the time it took to respond to the 911 call, had I driven farther into Bahia, I likely would have run out of life-force and would not have survived. But the triage team didn't give up on me. I had angels on my shoulder—the medical staff did not declare me DOA.

Hospital doctors and staff assessed me quickly: I was in critical condition—far worse than the community hospital could handle.

They stabilized me, and air-lifted me to Marin General Hospital, where a combination of magnificent medical skills and marvelous miracles waited for me. Angels were there, too.

Still unconscious (but obviously unwilling to die) it seems I did everything I could do to stay in the world of the living, even though I'd flat-lined twice during the procedures. Master surgeons Miguel Delgado Jr. and Dr. John Keohane and their team, with the guidance of chief medical officer, Dr. Jonathan Levin, worked for over eleven hours non-stop to mend my injuries and literally screw me back together. They performed a miracle, and I'm reminded of that often. Looking back, it all seems like an episode of a medical television drama. They placed me under the care of an Olympian Medical Dream Team, who combined their hard-earned skills with unquenchable hope of creating another incredible life-saving miracle...all while I was fast asleep/comatose.

I WOKE UP IN THE HOSPITAL ON MAY 14. IT WAS A FEW MONTHS before my twenty-first birthday. I'd spent the past two-and-a-half weeks unconscious in a physician-induced coma. When I woke up, I didn't know who I was, where I was or why, or even who the people standing over me were. I didn't even recognize my mother. I couldn't remember my name. I had significant brain damage, to where I couldn't speak or read. I had a case of mild amnesia, but thankfully, there was no damage to my spine. I was aware of being awake in a hospital, and that there had been some kind of trauma. I knew I was alive.

I saw a long blue tube. I could hear it pumping air. I knew the tube was going into a hole in my throat. I had a patch over my right eye. My hands and arms didn't work, and I couldn't move or feel my right leg. In fact, I had no feeling anywhere in my body. I learned later

49

that they sedated me, first with Morphine and then with Demerol, to mask the intense pain.

This was my return to the world I thought I knew. After a while, when I became a bit more aware, I realized where I was. *Is it Doomsday? Kill me now! I'm a singer and I have a hole in my throat! Please, pull the plug and burn the body!* These thoughts and more ran through my mind, but I couldn't even cry out. My jaw was wired shut. I had a tracheotomy hole. I found out soon enough that there was also a G-tube in my stomach. There was a hole in my throat, a hole in my belly, and a hole in my brain where my memories were stored.

While staring into my mother's sad eyes, I heard someone say... "Hello Aaron. I'm Dr. Levin. How are you feeling?"

"#&^%!#&^%!" I thought.

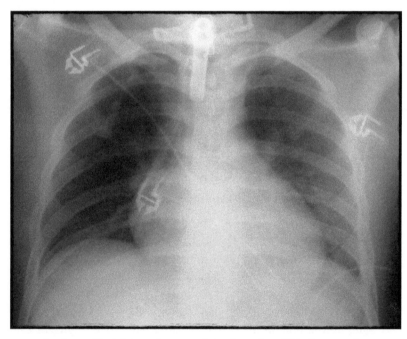

I woke up with a hole in my throat...my singing throat-throat. This Xray was taken during the first stages of my care at Novato Community Hospital, in April of 1998. In the photo you see a Tracheostomy tube, post and the ribcage area.

The ER surgeon on call the night of my accident happened (by another miracle) to be the president of the plastic surgery center of Northern California, outside of San Francisco, Dr. Miguel Delgado Jr. That dude does faces and was the best at it.

I was told that they used a then-current image of my father and a school photo of me in the tenth grade, aged sixteen, to perform reconstructive surgery on my face and skull. With these images, Dr. Delgado and his team assessed how my face would develop from age twenty to thirty as the healings and surgeries continued.

And... they got my eye back in... although I had no control of it. (But here's an update: After a full year of healing, I ended up gaining more control of my right eye.) The healing also improved my eyesight! I went from a vision score of 20/60 to 20/30. Now, twenty years later, I can do some fascinating stunts with my eye... onstage and for camera.

5:7 Profile Photo 2.0.

They should have amputated my foot when I got to Novato Community Hospital, and because they thought I didn't have any or proper insurance, my foot might have been amputated. Luckily, as I noted earlier, when they contacted my parents, my mother gave the hospital my father's medical insurance information. As I was a full-time college student, my dad's policy still covered me. This was a deciding moment for the rest of my life. I am alive, and walking, and dancing, and hiking, and jumping, and smiling, and massaging my physical foot right now as I write this, because my father worked his butt to the bone in his thirties, enough to provide ample medical coverage for his family. The American dream!

The doctors who attended to me right after my accident were miracle workers. I had Dr. Koehane as my reconstructive surgeon and Dr. Mendoza was my neurologist. They were sports medicine doctors who knew how to reshape feet to get a player back onto the field. They weren't building a wooden foot, so I could just get around. Build him back! Make him bigger, badder, stronger. Someone told me later that the actual words of my doctor were, "This guy is only twenty years old. We've got to give him a chance." And they drilled in and fixed my foot. There have been such painful moments in my recovery that really, all I wanted to do was amputate my foot myself. The deformity was too much to see daily. I was living on the edge of "limitations"—I could walk upstairs, but every step hurt like hell.

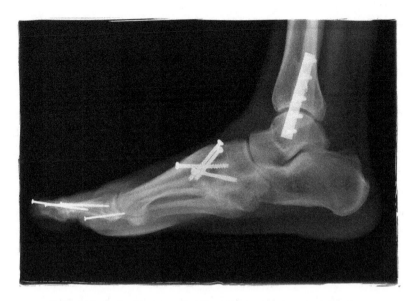

"A foot with nine lives" is a photo of an Xray taken in 2017 after a recent hammertoe correction surgery. The other hardware in the medial-cuneiform, liz franc, and ankle are from previous surgeries, dating back to 1998.

After the doctors at Marin General Hospital completed my surgeries, they prepared me for transfer to the famous Kentfield Rehabilitation Hospital in Larkspur, California. Over the course of the nineteen days spent at that amazing facility under the care of Dr. D. Doherty, I faced the reality of my injuries and the long-term effects they could have.

Naturally, I became fascinated by healing, and still am. I was full of gratitude and wanted to thank people, so I often did. 100% healing in every way! I had so many questions about death and dying, concepts of healing, religious views, and my new life as a "cripple." I was immobile and sedated, and as my brain continued to try making sense of the situation, there was only one question I could focus on: "What am I going to do with the rest of my life (besides undergo endless surgeries)?" It took two years of intense surgeries and stubbornness to get on my feet without a cast and to learn how to walk again. I felt that a wheelchair was never an option.

I was empty, afraid, alone, injured—and passionate to show others bravery. I seldom retreated into sadness out-loud, but I often did when I attempted to write in my journal. I couldn't wait to remove the pins and wires from my six-week-wired jaw. I wanted to sing again. I wanted to speak again. I WANTED, above all, to SMILE AGAIN! In all the photos that people shared with me to re-jog my memory, I noticed I was always smiling. "Aaron liked to smile," I said jokingly to my friend during a memorable hospital visit. Surprisingly —and luckily—despite all the injuries from head to toe, I kept every single tooth in my mouth, both on the top and bottom. I loved food so much, I guess. But, I digress.

First, I learned my name—and how to write it. Yes, learned. My brain needed to be re-conditioned with all the knowledge I had gained in the early years of my life. I had to learn my ABCs all over again, literally, even though I was one month away from graduating from my first three years of college. I could recognize the letter "A" but it had no meaning. I had just completed a Religious Studies course, studying complex subjects such as cat-ness; identifying with self—but for two weeks, I couldn't identify what a cat was.

Luckily, occupational and rehabilitation therapy didn't take as long as "going back to grammar school," but it was equally challenging. It was as if I'd never used my brain before. Think of it as Neo in the Matrix... and Dr. Doherty was my Morpheus.

Journal entry. June 5, 1998. I was suffering the loss of my ability to speak, sing, and smile. I was 20 years old. However, I praise the hard work of Kentfield Rehabilitation Center for my 3 week turnaround. I could write again! I believed I would smile again. But could I sing again?

I considered myself a scholar, so I knew how to learn. I knew I had a ways to go. I was a gentleman and could listen well. I was a musician and knew that with time and practice, I would only get better, and could eventually master... speech. Then, I could master melody.

On the afternoon of the accident, and for months prior, I had been rehearsing for a jazz choir concert with Ben Flint and the Harmony Corporation at Santa Rosa Junior College. Months later, I found out that because I was a no-show that night, they considered me a flake and a write-off. No one at my college knew what had happened for over a month—as I noted earlier, Santa Rosa is in Sonoma County, and the accident happened in Novato in Marin County. It was the end of the school year; almost summer. I was homeless. All of my teachers gave me "fails" or "incomplete," which I had to petition when I got back to school after the accident. I was able to test, later, to receive a grade—some other classes were a loss. More importantly, no one knew I had nearly died; few classmates, no teachers, coaches...I'd just disappeared.

The members of my choir were my closest buddies. We sang, ate, and worked together—and walked home together to sing s'more... in prep for a huge show. But because I spent most of my time at work, at school, and at the local dance clubs —and kept the rest of my life private, my coworkers, colleagues, and the bouncers at the club simply thought I was MIA. To Ben Flint, and all the rest—I'm so sorry I wasn't there to sing the parts we'd rehearsed so diligently. It breaks my heart to have let you down, even though I was busy trying to stay alive that night, and over the next month, trying to heal and deal with the trauma and the physical scars.

THEN THERE ARE THE PSYCHOLOGICAL SCARS.

I hate my face.

Correction: I hated my *new* face. I am blessed for the work Dr. Delgado so expertly performed. My wife thinks I'm the handsomest man in the world. My mother still sees her little baby boy, but not me. I see scars. I see damage. For example, I have little sensation in my lower lip. My bottom teeth punctured through it, severing many nerves. So, I mumble... sometimes. I mumble whenever I'm tired or unrested—as if the nerves just bail out on me. Add to that I have a condition in my right eye called sub-conjunctival hemorrhaging because of the blow-out fracture; it causes my eye to flare up red at random times. I looked like an addict. It took a lot of confidence to face my new face each day—every day since the day I woke from the coma and saw my new "self." I didn't want to wear my sunglasses at night (to hide my eye)...I wanted my old eye back.

"Face the facts - Face the face" On *June 14, 1998 I was 6 weeks into recovery, my jaw was no longer wired shut and today the trach-tube was removed.*

I was traumatized. But I was patient—and I was a good patient. I followed the directions the doctors gave me to a "T." I had to practice speaking again. It felt like an art form—as if I was learning to paint like da Vinci overnight. I had to learn how to create vowels, how to identify consonants—I had to re-learn my life, one day at a time.

First, I had to accept the notion that everything happens for a reason... and to believe that, I simply needed to meditate. But I didn't know how to meditate. I believed that anything is possible... except meditation, perhaps. Under the direction of the amazing Dr. D. Doherty at the Kentfield Rehabilitation Center, my occupational therapy team taught me how to set my body back in motion. Dr. Doherty tried to help me learn to calm my mind: to rest and allow my body time to heal. I was a busy bee, and my brain waves had always been extremely active. I needed to stop. And the moment I did... stop... I felt as if I'd started.

It was in that moment of... let's call it zero gravity... with no weight on my shoulders, that I could construct a clear path to recovery. I calmed the chatter and released all the fears and inhibitions that told me I could not heal or would never sing again. Instead, I fell into the abyss of non-thought for the first time in my old and new life. I saw everything so clearly.

I said, "Yes, I will."

———

IT REMINDS ME OF THE WORDS TO THAT GOOD-OL' SONG, "THE Itsy-Bitsy Spider" ... Yes! All true! As I reflect on the song lyrics themselves, the message was obvious, and the life lesson became ingrained. Repetitive children's songs and nursery rhymes shaped my path to positive healing—and paid off. Hearing words of encouragement and hope, and having a logical goal to move forward and an attitude of "YES, I WILL SURVIVE!" really works! I learned resiliency growing up. I knew that if for one moment my mind quit —I'd quit. I did not ... I went up the spout again.

I chose not to allow the accident to deviate me from my path to success. I had the will to live. I had the love of friends and family and that great team who supported me: teachers, professors, doctors, and nurses from all over California... they filled my soul with that now-infamous campaign slogan used by former President Barack Obama: "YES, YOU CAN!"

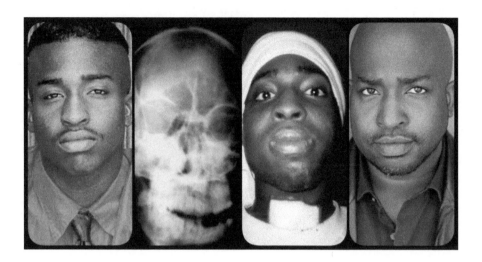

Act 6
IF YOU BELIEVE IN... HOPE

I'm a fan of survival shows like "Alone," "Survivorman," and "Naked and Afraid." These shows all have the same theme: Someone is lost in the wilderness and wants to stay alive. I was the same. After my accident, the world was new to me, yet familiar enough to navigate. I wanted to live! I needed food, water, and shelter, and I needed ongoing medical care.

But the wilderness that was my world was not filled with dangerous creatures or poisonous plants—it was filled with beeping machines, intravenous drips, and medical devices that I still don't know the name of. Then, that endless sequence of surgeries. On the fortieth day, June 5, there was still a tube in my neck. They tried to remove the tracheotomy, but as my body had healed, it had grown into the trach. So, I went home with that tube in my neck, then went back on June 12 to have a minor surgery to have it removed. I was nervous, eager to know what would happen once they dislodged it. *Would I be able to sing again?* I was awake for the surgery. Imagine this: An aspiring singer, staring at the tools on the operating table, hoping for a miracle as the doctor struggles to pull a tube out of his throat. When it popped out, I immediately tried to speak. There was an uncontrollable rush of air blowing out of the hole, but no words. I gasped for air and could only feel it rushing into the hole in my neck. I cried.

I believed, for just an instant, that I would never sing again. They stitched me up, gave me antibiotics and instructions, and sent me on my way. My mother was there. We were silent on the way back home. I had a hole in my throat...shoot me now.

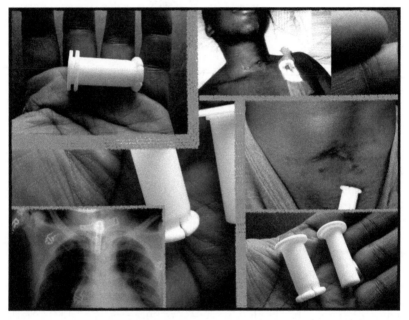

This is a photo of the hole where my voice used to be. *April & June, 1998.*

After forty nights and forty days—literally—they released me from the hospital. I moved back home with my parents. I was on bed rest until my wounds healed. My mother became my night nurse, and they hired someone to help during the day. My loving family spent the following two weeks tending to my wounds and driving me to and from surgery, all the while tending to their tears and adjusting their pocketbooks. They believed I could heal, and I could feel it.

Still, this is the most painful part of my story and my heart breaks today just thinking about those days. Mom and Dad gave me a bed, and Mom cared for me. My foot had to be placed in a whirlpool with Betadine and warm water three times a day for the massive pressure ulcer on my foot. My trach wound had to be wiped clean regularly. With my jaw wired shut, I couldn't move, so we didn't talk much. I was medicated heavily, taking fifteen to twenty pills a day to save my life. I slept—a lot. Showers were horrific—I did not have the strength to hold my body up. With my injuries, I was susceptible to osteomyelitis, a bone infection, and I could die from it—the doctors had warned me repeatedly that it was a real risk. All the while, bursts of painful memories continued to arise; I couldn't control them.

WE WERE ALL IN SHOCK. MY CAR-ACCIDENT MONKEY-WRENCHED many peoples' lives. I'd been one month away from college graduation and just days away from my twenty-first birthday. I'd left home for college at seventeen, with no intention of returning. Now, I was an adult, independent, but in the most vulnerable state imaginable. I was back living with my parents when I'd been just one month from tackling the entire world! I didn't want to hear: "You can't... you won't... you may never... most likely not...," or the emphatic phrase, "While you live in my house, you will follow my rules."

I wasn't able to raise my arms yet. I could see out of my left eye only, and hoped my damaged eye would heal. They fused my joints with metal. I could barely walk. I had shrunk from 175 to 135 pounds. I had learned somewhere that laughter is healing. I needed a good laugh. Could I smile again? My jaw was locked—so I set a goal to smile again starting on June 12, 1998—the day they were going to pull the pins out of my teeth, just above the gums, that was holding my jaw in place.

Aaron Turner, Jr.

After three weeks of bedrest, I was still unrested. And I was bored. I couldn't help around the house. I was learning to speak again and to recognize the alphabet. My Mom wanted to sit and read the Bible with me, but I didn't feel like reading.

I'd been blind-sided, the accident had ripped my life away from me —I wanted it back. So, I rebelled. I admit, I became intolerable. I was healing *my way,* and I didn't want anyone else's oppinion in my ears... including my parents', although they were trying their best to help me heal. I had brain damage, memory loss, and was on enough medication to sedate a young bear... or so I often felt. I forgot how to be human. I stopped believing in humanity.

My Moms Take (abridged)

Sent to me on May 12, 2013; Mothers Day

 It was approximately 1p and my husband and I had just returned from having breakfast with our daughter, Letitia. I heard my answering machine beeping and went to check my messages. I had one message and it went something like this "This call is for Mr. or Mrs. Turner. This is the Emergency room of Novato Community Hospital. Please call our office at 707-###-####." I immediately went weak in the knees and had to sit down. I said to my husband, it's Aaron, something has happened to him. My husband said "Oh, Lord".

My hands were shaking as I dialed the number not knowing exactly what I was going to hear on the other line. I knew it had to be my son since I had just left my daughter and the message said it was about 11am in the morning on my answering machine.

I called the Emergency room and said "this is Mrs. Turner and someone left a message for me to call your office". The person on the other end said "Just a moment please" and she then returned and said "Do you have a son named Aaron?". I said "yes", and at that moment my stomach was so queasy I almost threw up waiting to hear her next words.

She then said "We have your son here, he's been in an automobile accident. Hold on and Dr.... will speak with you.

A doctor came on the line and started telling me Aaron's condition. He indicated he was in ICU and they were waiting for the plastic surgeon to arrive. He also informed me that he was being transported to Marin General Hospital.

He gave me the address and he advised me not to come right then as I probably would not be able to take Aaron's appearance. He then began to tell me how the steering wheel had smashed his face and lower jaw so that he was terribly disfigured, he said he had an orbital blowout fracture of his eye, I believe it was the right eye. He also indicated he had fractured foot and all five of his toes on his right foot. I was devastated!

Immediately after speaking with him, we called Letitia and told her what had happened, she just couldn't believe it! We called my sisters Missionary Helen & Missionary Alpha, Aaron's[Sr.] Nephew, Pastor Kelly to begin a prayer chain going, we then jumped back in the car and raced to Marin General Hospital.

When we got there Aaron was already in surgery. Many family members came to the waiting room, so much that we had to be asked to be quiet. My niece Lorraine & her husband Clinton, his sister, his other Auntie Zelma and her husband Gilbert and some others. As we were waiting, one of the nurses came in and said there was a phone call for me. When I picked up the phone in the waiting room, it was the lady that helped save Aaron's life at the scene of the accident. It was her tree that his car had struck in her front yard! Through tears I thanked her for her help and for calling 911 for my son. I told her that I know it was God that had her there at that moment! She went on to ask how he was doing, told her he was still in surgery she said she would be praying for him.

More than 11 hours later, Dr. Delgado came out and told us he was done, to our relief, he said he looked amazing from what he started with. He said Aaron's face was grotesque.
  He had no idea what Aaron looked like so he was reconstructing him like the bionic man. He put his eye back in its socket, he said he did not know if he would be able to see or not until he awakened out of his coma. We thanked and praised him for saving our son's face. He did a phenomenal job!

We stayed at the hospital all night and was able to actually go in and see him somewhere in the wee hours of the morning. They warned us of what we were going to see. When we walked in Aaron was lying there all hooked up to machines, his face was swollen to no end, about the size of...I can't even describe how huge it was. My husband and I took his hand and began to pray for him, as tears came from us both. All his dad could say was "Oh Lord, oh man". He doesn't show his emotions very often, but you could clearly see he was visibly shaken at this sight.

We drove back and forth every day for the next two weeks, talking to Aaron, holding his hand, telling him we loved him and wanted him to wake up. We were waiting for him to wake up. I couldn't eat, nothing stayed in my stomach it went right through me. I lost 20 lbs in less than 10 days. That was the most horrific time in my life! I never want to experience that again. It was awful.

Then one day as we had just gotten home, the phone rang. It was Aaron's nurse, she said he can't talk as he has a trach but she was going to put the phone to his ear. She also said that he wrote "I LOVE YOU, DAD & TISH". Of course this brought many tears to my eyes as I knew he was going to be alright since he recognized who I was. Praise God! My son is going to be alright.

As I sit here writing this note, 15 years later, it still gives me a queasy stomach and tears, and every time we drive by the Atherton turnoff, my stomach still does a little flip flop. Aaron has come a long, long ways. I know he was brought back from death for a purpose that only he can fulfill. Keep on pushing for it Aaron, you will fulfill it. I love you and always will be there for you.

Love, your Mom

MY MOTHER AND FATHER WERE BOTH FRIGHTENED, BUT PERHAPS didn't understand that I had a little brain damage. Things were still foggy. I had temporary amnesia. Drugged with medication, I was scared and my mind was stuck in repeat mode—thoughts of all the events that had been going on in my life just before the car accident kept circling through my thoughts: *Why had this happened to me? I wasn't a bad person. I wasn't doing anything bad—I was a good person, a twenty-year-old kid in college, just about to graduate.* Leading up to the moment of impact, I'd been in party-celebration mode, and I was stuck in the cycle of striving for success! I wanted to win, and I knew how. So, my need to be victorious in all that I did led to a conflict between myself and my parents.

Add to all of this that I would rather have died than not spend time with my then-sweetheart. I didn't grasp the fact that I was forty pounds shy of when she'd seen me last. I had only one working foot and needed care 24/7. The massive deformity in my face was not a part of the wedding photo she'd perhaps had in mind. But I couldn't understand that... I was damaged. I needed counselling to deal with the trauma and heartache. I was young. Our relationship did not last, and I had to make it on my own without her. I began to become introverted and depressed.

But my family believed that the only true counselling I needed would come from the King James version of the Bible. I was twenty years old and trying not to hear that. My folks were trying not to hear my "No." They felt I could find the answers to my turmoil in scripture, and when I was well enough, they left me alone with a Bible and cable TV. They needed time to heal too. There wasn't much else they could do for me.

We were all hurting. We were all scared. My father really wanted me to read my Bible. At the time, I couldn't understand why I needed to read the Bible when all I wanted to do was talk to the girl I was dating and to see my friends. I missed them so much. They scolded me for not putting God first. My parents believed that if I'd died in that car and I wasn't yet "saved" they didn't know whether I was going to go to heaven or straight to hell. I ended up arguing with my dad over the time I spent not reading the verses, versus the time I spent on the phone talking to my friends. Out of frustration, perhaps, he unplugged the phone one day. So, I refused to read the scriptures.

"Talent and Devotion". *June 5, 2010. Aaron's singing with his family-four [left to right] Aaron Jr., singing, Gloria, singing, Aaron Sr., electric guitar, and Letitia, on drums., at Hilltop Apostolic Church, in Lower Lake, Ca.*

"My house, my rules." If I wasn't willing to follow their guidelines, my parents said, I'd need to leave and find someplace else to heal. It had only been two weeks since they had released me from hospital care. Mom had cared for me until she had to return to work. We were all healing... but looking back now, I wonder, did our family ever heal?

I took my crutches, my backpack with my medicines, my journal, my eye-patch, and a broken pager that held my phone numbers. I called a friend to pick me up, and I began the second wave of healing...on the streets.

Over the following two years, I was a nomad. By choice. I look back and think that I may not have been completely sane enough to have made that decision, but it was mine to own. Sometimes I slept on the streets of Santa Rosa. More often than not, though, I had a sofa or a spare room to crash in. To heal in. There were friends and colleagues around when I needed them. As I was to others before this turn of events. And on the days I had no support, I found refuge in a box or in an abandoned car. I was healing in so many locations, also in so many places on my body. I had to avoid infections that could lead to a terminal illness—I was always concerned about osteomyelitis when I was sleeping outside, behind a Macy's loading dock in the downtown mall. I wanted to survive no matter what—if for no other reason than to tell you this story: Anything Is Possible!

"A Great Rescue". *April, 1998. I am being pulled from the wreckage.*

The only place in Santa Rosa where I had access to everything from clean showers to warm classrooms was the Junior College. I was already receiving grants, scholarships, and a student loan. Why not ask for some life help so I could get back on my feet—or foot? Almost a year after the accident, the pressure ulcer on my right foot needed a skin graft. A skin graft procedure would harvest healthy skin from my thigh or buttocks, and graft it to the injury, using mineral oils and metal staples.

Nonetheless, I had open sores on that foot, and they were painful—physically and emotionally. I could barely move my jaw, and my eye had a prism in it. It's hard when you are pushing yourself in a wheelchair across campus, with one eye, with only ten minutes to get to class. I never wanted to be late. That was against my life principles—to ever be late to anything. I gained newfound respect for those suffering from permanent limitations; to which we all are subjected to at any time.

THERE WERE CLEAR STEPS TO RECOVERY. BUT WITHOUT HELP FROM SRJC, I would not recover, so there was a dire need for me to pass my courses. Where there's a will, there's a way, I believed in myself. I'd done it before. I was so grateful that they helped me with housing. Food was accessible. Water was free. The cells in my brain were connecting again. But I wasn't truly ready for class yet. I was still grieving my losses—the life I had known, my physical freedom, my loss of functionality, everything. Life had broken my heart.

I trudged through the many stages of grief, as one would expect of a twenty-year-old who had just lost his dreams. I was still pushing forward, sometimes a couch-surfer, other times living on the street. Over two years, I learned resiliency. I learned to cope with my pain. I never lost hope. I was willing to heal, but the healing process did not come easily. In fact, I know pain like many people know sunshine... for to this day, there is not a day that I play in the sunshine without suffering pain.

Pain medication was affecting my life negatively, hindering my self-care. I was instructed to take so many pills a day—almost all for pain, but some for infection. The adverse reactions outweighed the positive effects, by far. In order to be pain-free, did I also need to be dizzy, nauseous, and constipated? No. Nor did I want to numb my brain. I would not use the opioids that were available in the late-90s.

71

Aaron Turner, Jr.

Instead I used over-the-counter medication like Advil, Tylenol and, Aleve, except during major surgeries...for those I was prescribed Demerol, Percocet, Vicodin, Percodan, Ultram, or other experimental pain meds offered at the time. But, after surgery, I wanted to be more present, even in pain, to take in the lessons of my healing journey. The more I moved, the less I needed medication. In

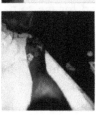

my case, it didn't hurt to heal, if fact it felt rejuvenating. I used physical movement to better heal my injuries.

I chose to dance because I believed it could heal me.

Polaroid Photo. June 14, 1998. A massive pressure ulcer, open, on the heel and mid-cuneiform area of my right foot, caused by a very hot car engine and immense pressure.

Performing Live, at The Imperial,
Vancouver, B.C. for "Instruments of Change",
2015.
Photo by James Healy

Act 7
IF YOU BELIEVE IN... THE HEALING ARTS

L ike I said, I never gave up hope. My new goal was education. I returned to school to begin my journey toward knowledge. I was at SRJC from June 1995 to May 2003, even while I was attending SSU 2001 to 2003. I loved and still love learning; classrooms, knowledge, and conversations.

But, I also needed money. I didn't find my first job until the summer of 1999. I lived in the dorms at the Junior College during that summer, and worked at the YMCA Performing Arts Camp down the street. No more sofa-surfing. No more sleeping outside the Santa Rosa Plaza. No more drinking coffee all night long at a twenty-four-hour diner. No more phone calls to exes to get a good night's sleep. Instead, introducing children to the arts saved me. I was a camp counsellor with thirty kids aged seven to twelve, singing songs and learning theatre—they were respecting me for who I was. None of them even noticed my injuries, only my spirit within. It revived me! I was healing by teaching the arts. I can still remember the "Y" cheer.

Aaron Turner, Jr.

MY PASSION FOR MY FIRST JOB WAS INSPIRED BY MY FIRST NIGHT out. On January 29, 1999, I watched the friends I was living with at the time perform in a theatrical production at Santa Rosa Junior College's Burbank Auditorium, called "Stand-up Tragedy." Jeremy, John, JJ, and Carla, to name a few, were co-starring in this production. That show and their performance inspired my career in the performing arts. Not only were they actors, but they were also rappers and singers. I was in awe. I sat at the back of the theatre because I didn't want my face exposed to a crowd—I was broken. I was in a wheelchair, so they sat me in an aisle seat for a person with a disability. Through my one good eye, I saw the most beautiful thing I'd ever seen in my life: live theatre! I watched the actors—the people I knew. I heard them sing live onstage as they did in rehearsal. They moved and danced in vibrant color—it was larger than life! I felt like I was in it, like it was in me. It was like a film, but I could feel heat from the stage lights; the sound speaker was literally beneath my feet! It was real. It was live! I felt alive again!

I want to do that! I want to do it forever. Through the entire production, I could feel my synapses firing into my legs, into the hole in my throat, into my hands. I wanted to clap my hands together, sing out loud, and dance. I was born again... oh, to be on stage! I was hooked. And then it happened: As the play resolved and the final musical number came on, I recognized the musical intro of the backing track. I'd heard that song before.

Then voices followed, singing, "Something wicked—this way's comin'... something wicked, this way is coming..." and I began singing along silently. That's me... I burst into tears! That's my voice!

In the recording, I'm singing with Jonathan Jones and John Willis, and the music had been written by our friend, and musical mastermind, Chris Sears. We had recorded the number in the studio months prior; it was the first time I'd sung since the doctors had removed the trach. And now, for the first time, I was hearing my "new" voice on a big stage. At that moment, it overwhelmed me with hope. I said to myself, before I die again, I'm going to do that. I'm going to get up on that stage, and it's going to be my voice, live, in this theatre. *That's me from now on!... I will perform with or without my foot or my right eye—I believe wholeheartedly that I can. "Dear God, can I please do this for the rest of my life?"*

7.2 "My Ticket to Ride"

The following semester I moved out of the dorm room and secured a studio apartment. I hobbled into the Santa Rosa Junior College Theatre Arts Department and said, "I'd like to become a theatre person." General auditions were coming up that Saturday, and they handed me the information I needed. After my audition, the faculty members looked at my questionnaire and asked, amongst other things, "What else do you do?" I replied: "Well, I sing. I used to dance and play a little piano." They said, "We have no specific roles for you this season, but we need help with the sound department." I was curious...I liked "sound." I was happy they didn't say no, nothing at all for you, sorry... quite the opposite. So, in my first week in the department, they introduced me to a man named Theo.

Aaron Turner, Jr.

THEO BRIDANT RAN THE TECHNICAL SIDE OF THE THEATRE. HE was awesome! Brilliant! Easy to get along with and my perfect mentor on stage life, namely *sound*. When we met, he was wearing a tool belt with jeans and a dirty shirt. He walked up to me with a smile and said something cool like: "What's up, man?" We became close friends from that point on. Theo was noticeably taller than me —about six foot four, and we looked cool standing there side by side. In retrospect, it was great to stand again—free from the wheelchair. Nonetheless, I looked up to Theo, and said, "teach me anything you want me to learn—I'll listen." And I also told him that I was a little broken and beat up. I'm sure he could notice, but it didn't matter with sound so much, as I'd discover later.

He taught me sound. Literally. He taught me from scratch—the difference between mono and stereo, wave editing, microphone setups, and sound designing for stage (e.g., the crickets and the cars, the FX and the music, and the strategic speaker placement). I told him I could write and sing songs for the productions coming up... and he and the directors gave me the opportunity to do just that. This was the turnaround moment of my life. They gave me the chance to do my best at something. I was smiling again.

It turned out to be epic for the entire theatre department. The production we worked on, "Watermelon Nights," was a staging of Greg Sarris's novel. It was based on the performing style of a San Francisco theatre company called Word for Word. They stage and act out every word of short stories as opposed to plays. Both the written work and the theatre style was magnificent. In my opinion it was the epitome of bringing words to life; page to stage. And I got to be a part of it—fresh out of the gate!

Theo and I designed the sound together, but he let me write and record all the underscores, voice-overs, and the theme song for the show. I designed everything from scratch rather than pulling music from archives. In the closing number, I sang my original song, "Can't

Be in Two Places," every night, for every show, with a microphone in my hand, screws in my feet, a hole in my throat, one eye, and brain damage. I was the sound board operator during the show, and at the end, I would walk onstage singing:

Let me choose my own path, to find my way,

even if it takes me through thick and thin,

You don't want me to go, but I know my destination,

And inside is where I'm going to begin...

Give me a chance, let me decide

Wait until I make up my mind,

I'll still be a man, even if I'm not with my tribe

'Cause I can't be in two places...at one time.

THE APPLAUSE AWED ME... THEN, A STANDING OVATION. I'D DONE it... from page to stage! An "Opening Night"! As the lights dimmed, I exited. Later, as I celebrated with the cast, I thought about my contributions to the performance. I'd found my tribe. I'd found my calling. All and all, it was a grand production. I knew then that anything is possible. I believed!

We continued the run of the show. Night after night. I learned to set up, and I learned to strike. I was building sets for future shows, and programming the sound effects in our current show. I was working; I was passing my classes; I was rehabilitating through activity. Theatre! Music! Love!

"Watermelon Nights" continued with rave reviews, awards, and so much recognition that it helped set the tone for many theatre productions over the next three years. We were invited to a national competition hosted by The Kennedy Center in Washington, D.C.

Aaron Turner, Jr.

The event was being held at the University of Las Vegas, and I was being judged, along with the others. It was so exciting! And afterwards, the adjudicators nominated me to compete in the Sound category. Other designers were nominated for their designs in Costume, Lights, as well as several Actors...for acting, of course. They recognized me for my Original Music Composition, and I also won the Kate Drain Lawson award for my design. This was more than I'd ever imagined two years earlier when I'd seen my first opening act during "Stand Up Tragedy." I'd become a theatre person. I was healing.

Photo taken during the pre-production of "Farewell Angelina" at Santa Rosa Junior College. 2002. *pictured here with instructor/director/dept. chair Leslie McCauley, and Anita Silva, at Waldorf recording studio. Sonoma State University.

One year later, I was asked to design sound and compose for another Word For Word styled production, this time from the short story "Halfway Diner," written by John Sayles. Leslie McCauley directed it. She brought her best team together, a stellar cast of multi-cultural Actors, and on stage we all created magic! Many Actors from the ensemble, and some designers like myself, were invited back to the American College Theater Festival to compete again. Although there were so many wonderful take-aways from those three days at

Fresno State, notably I was the sound design winner for my contributions to "Halfway Diner." I wrote some of my best music in that production, set to the blues, hip-hop, and R&B. Santa Rosa Junior College. Theatre Arts Department was a diamond in the rough—and I was lucky to have found it. And now I found my voice again!

7:4 *Sound Design and Original Music Composition for the stage.*

I SWITCHED PROGRAMS AND CONTINUED ADVANCING THROUGH THE theatre curriculum. I started with Introduction to Theatre with Leslie McCauley—I truly thank her for all of my onstage successes. We ended three years later with classes like Advanced Acting and Production for the Stage. I was hooked on her teaching style from day one. There was so much potential in stage work; from writing to producing. Leslie showed me that there was obvious opportunity for me. She called me a "post-modern artist," at the time, and I was so honoured. There was a place in the world for people like me.

Maryanne Scozzari, the chair of the department, gave me the support I needed to heal while exploring the craft. She helped to design my learning in line with my strengths and weaknesses, namely my foot limitations. I completed the three years theatre arts acting program at the J.C. in 2001 and transferred immediately to Sonoma State University. Straight out of the gate, after my first audition, I landed the lead male role as Tamino in Mozart's "The Magic Flute."

81

Aaron Turner, Jr.

Yes, an Opera! It is one thing to be nervous and insecure about singing opera, but I also had a hole in my throat... *How am I going to sing opera?* I hadn't learned yet that I didn't need to do the thinking. SSU instructor/music conductor Lynne Morrow and director Amanda McTigue, also the adaptor of Mozart's libretto, saw something in me I would only discover later. I was a lead actor—but mere years ago, I was barely alive. But I was alive on stage. Every night and for every matinee, I shared a stage with a massive, talented ensemble of professional opera singers (like my co-star who played Pamina—she was flawless). I felt so lucky! Together we brought Mozart's newly re-inspired music to a large, satisfied audience.

Note: we began rehearsals on Sept. 11, 2001.

7.5 "A magical moment in my life". *2001. The Magic Flute at Sonoma State University [Tamino];* Mozart's opera blends the ridiculous and the sublime. *This article was salvaged from a review in the Press Democrat Newspaper.*

There were posters with reviews around the walls. My star was rising.

Along the way, my foot collapsed again. Just as I had begun to feel normal. I was dancing to the rhythm of life, and perhaps because of it, I developed a large, painful bone spur in the cuneiform region of my foot. I had another important surgery in 1999 to correct it. Soon after that surgery, it collapsed again. In 2000, a different surgeon, Dr. Russell Bodner, did the final reconstructive surgery on my foot. He said, "We're going to redesign your foot and place it in a walking position. But this is it. This is the last surgery. We recommend no more due to scar tissue and soft tissue damage." Then he said, "If this surgery doesn't work, we'll have to make some adjustments. You may wake up to an amputated foot." Yes, at the ankle.

I didn't take any of this for granted: they had given me a second chance, a second attempt at life, after death. I couldn't continue on the path I was headed in... I couldn't be a culinary king and I had lost my desire to be a pop musician. I needed to find a new profession—but what? I knew there'd be a long recovery, as lower extremity injuries need time and elevation to heal, so I needed something sedentary. But all of my previous training had been in "hustle." I'd been a server at numerous restaurants, a courtesy clerk at two grocery stores, collected golf carts in Hidden Valley, and then worked at Sears...where could a student work without two good feet?

I applied and was hired at Bank of America, in Santa Rosa, as a teller. There was a stool, so I could stand or sit when I needed to. I did need to sit and stand for every shift. I also rented a one-bedroom apartment, near the bank, a block from Coddingtown Mall, so I didn't have to commute. This transition was the catalyst that led to my enrollment in theater arts at Sonoma State University... I had a day job so now I could take the necessary night classes and perhaps perform in the late evenings. I was great at customer service. I planned to transfer to another branch if I ever moved. For that reason the bank job lasted two years, until I graduated from Sonoma State University, and was my last job in Santa Rosa. In May 2003 I walked, yes walked, with my peers in a ceremony to celebrate our well-earned achievements. I graduated with a Bachelor of Arts Degree in Liberal Studies, with a concentration on performing arts and a minor in sound and audio engineering.

7.6 As Prince Tamino. 2001.

After graduation, I moved to San Francisco for a sound design internship at Berkeley Repertory Theatre (BRT). It was there that I first became immersed in the professional theatre world. Big stages. Actors from all over the world—and directors, designers, and not to mention the awe of Berkeley, California. Thank you Rachel and William for teaching me the ropes and welcoming me in.

During the early days of my internship at BRT, a fellow intern asked me: "Why aren't you on stage?" I was like: "Awhhhhh man... like, my face? And my foot is kinda jacked up... I don't know."

"So! Why aren't you on stage?" Then he named a long list of actors and performers with disabilities, like having only one ear, or a prosthetic leg, and, of course, being blind!

I didn't have any excuses. It was time for headshots.

Before I left the building that day, the production manager of BRT approached me. I was standing with my supervisor. "How are you enjoying your internship?" he asked.

I thought it was a shakedown. I replied, "Great!" and praised the brilliance of the Head of Sound and AV. I was so nervous... until he cut to the chase with: "We have a production coming up with eight black male roles, and we need someone to understudy... and you have a theatre background too, right, like acting?"

I replied, "Yes, I sure do."

"Great!" he said, and then asked, in front of my supervisor, "Have you ever done any understudying?"

"What's that?" I asked.

He replied, "Great—you'll work out just fine!"

He said "OK," to my boss ... and left.

I understudied the roles of respected actors Derek Lee Weeden and Jacob Ming Trent, in the epic staging of "The Continental Divide: Daughters of the Revolution and Mother's Against" at Berkeley Repertory Theatre. Two full productions in rep, otherwise running on two separate stages, simultaneously. And it moved fast. The ensemble was stellar, playing multiple characters in both productions. I'm talking about the best acting I had ever seen. And from this experience, the actor Aaron Junior Turner was ignited. They were spectacular! I could not compare nor could I believe, at first, that this opportunity came to me. Week after week, show after show, I began to see myself on the Roda stage at BRT, in front of an audience, and for the rest of my life doing so! I manifested this—I believe this now. It was like an advanced acting course or a master's class in San Francisco Bay Area Theater-ing. I was "in-production" – I was out of the hospital for good. I was on my way!

85

Aaron Turner, Jr.

ACTF CONTINUED FROM PAGE NINE: *ACTF puts production design on display*

finalists. The Santa Rosa Junior College production competed for both costume and sound design. Sound designer Aaron "Junior" Turner said that "'Watermelon Nights' is a coming of age story about a twenty-two year-old mixed-blood Native American male." Turner went on to explain that "Watermelon Nights" was not performed traditionally. Unlike other plays, "Nights" had one scene— Johnny Chapter 5— spoken word for word.

Turner wrote and performed the theme song "Can't Be in Two Places". The chorus beautifully expresses the distress felt by the main character without even having seen the play performed: "Give me a chance/ Let me decide/ Wait until I make up my mind/ I'll still be a man, even if I'm not with my tribe/ Cause I can't be in two places at one time."

"ACTF brought together the best of the best—not to compete, but to collaborate." Turner said, expressing his feelings about the Festival. "ACTF has inspired me as a musician. There's no place I'd rather be than amongst my peers."

American College Theater Festival. *April, 2000. Sound design by Turner, Jr. A. University of Las Vegas, Nevada, campus newspaper.*

SRJC theater hits it big with *Halfway Diner*

James Galimo
Head Copy Editor

The SRJC Theater Arts is proud to bring you *Halfway Diner*, adapted from a short story by John Sayles. It was a very unusual show; it was not really adapted into a play so much as it was a group of very talented actors and actresses telling us the story, word for word as Sayles wrote it.

This may require a bit of explaining, so here's how it worked: The story was divided into lines as they rehearsed, so all of the narrative (the actions, thoughts and expressions of the characters) were spoken aloud by the actors as they performed.

When this was explained to us before the show began by the director, I thought this would make the show rather dull. I couldn't have been more wrong.

The actors used the narrative to express their emotions in a way that regular spoken lines couldn't have done alone.

The show began with a hip-hop song called "Meet Me Halfway," by local rap group High Intent and Aaron Junior Turner, who also played a couple different characters in the show. This was immediately followed by a blues song, called "Halfway Home," written and performed by Turner. The blues song flowed right into the

story, which was about a busload of women who were travelling to a prison to visit their husbands, boyfriends and sons.

As the show progressed, we learned that many of the women have been m[...] this long trek over an[...] throughout the years[...] Relationships formed between ma[...] them as well as som[...] mosity. Thanks to the[...] tive, you're able to tel[...] they feel about each[...] their situations and th[...] they're on their way t[...]

A new girl name[...] (Jessicah Larson), joi[...] we gain understand[...] the situation as she d[...] During the trip, the[...] at an eatery dubbed- ....Halfway Diner."

After they arrive at the prison, it is learned that a fight broke out between two prisoners whose girlfriends are friends with each other. This puts a wedge between the two and becomes one of the more interesting plotlines in the show.

Josh Rice, who plays multiple characters

in the show said it could be "very trying at times" to portray multiple characters.

Looking at what I thought was a skeleton

Halfway Diner, now in production at SRJC, presents its audience with a complex and fascinating glimpse into its characters.

of a stage set, I have to admit I didn't think the show would be interesting at all. The set just looked so bland. That was before I fully understood the idea behind it.

The set was constructed the way it was to make it easy to change the scene from one location to another. This was accomplished by simply moving all of the chairs around.

The second reason goes [...] the narrative. As [...]w progressed, the [...]ecame filled by the [...]way through, it [...] even a set to me [...]re. I could almost [...]y see the bus, the [...]d, of course, the [...]y diner itself.

[...]e McCauley di-[...] this absolutely [...]d cast, some of [...] worked with [...]ley before in last *Watermelon*

Together the cast and crew put on a fine show. I wholeheartedly recommend that you see this show before it closes after this weekend.

Halfway Diner will run Oct. 12 to 15 at 8 p.m. with daytime shows on Saturday and Sunday at 2 p.m. Admission is $10 general and $7 for students and seniors.

Halfway Diner made the news. 2001. Actor, Singer, Songwriter and Sound Designer

"Halfway Diner" 2000

So, I was building a life in the arts. I was up for a new challenge. And there it was: "The Continental Divide." This experience was just the beginning of a good string of productions starting in San Francisco and ending in Canada. How I got to Canada you'll discover as you continue on—sadly the timeline overlaps and a few surprises may be spoiled.

Nonetheless, during "The Continental Divide," I was struck by the acting bug, and when the show wrapped, I continued to audition for roles around the Bay Area. I played a longshoreman in the play "Anna Christie," worked with the African American Shakespeare Company, had minor roles in other productions, and did sound design for local theatre companies on the side.

I booked a role as Sneaky Pete in "Beggar's Holiday" at Marin Theatre Company, working with Christopher Jackson ("The Lion King," "Hamilton"), James Monroe ("Aladdin," "Sweeney Todd"), and other amazing theatre stars. There were lots of singing and tons of dancing. Because I was also a dancer before the car accident, I used muscle memory to return to the dance floor but this time I was dancing on stage with professional dancers, at a Broadway caliber. I was not up to par. I literally had two left feet—my right foot was so deformed and mutilated, it looked like I had two left feet. Yet, I rehearsed every day on those two left feet with those Broadway stars! The local newspaper interviewed me about my return to stage —an article you can still find in a google search.[1]

"BEGGAR'S HOLIDAY" WAS MY ABSOLUTE FAVOURITE THEATRE production while living in California. It stretched my new "me" to its limit...at the time. Literally, stretching and flexibility were key to my being able to dance six nights a week. So was a positive attitude and a "never-give-up," loving approach to life. People helped too, namely seasoned cast members who sat down to share advice about my future as a Thespian. I determined that musical theatre seemed like a natural transition. I set a goal to sing... I didn't set any limitations as to where I could sing. In smaller and local productions I'd train for bigger stages and grander roles. I'd gain experience and build my resume before ever attempting New York City, for example. And so I began.

At the time, I lived in an apartment close to a karaoke bar, and it gave me easy access to a stage where I could sing. One night I met an amazing woman, Jennifer... I'll talk about our outstanding adventures together in the next Act. But for now, suffice it to say that meeting her changed my life forever. Not long after we met, we discovered we were both longing to experience more nature, more freedom, and a new way of life... so, long story short, a year later, we moved to Canada.

When Jen and I arrived in Vancouver, B.C. in 2005, I immersed myself in the theatre world immediately. I was involved in the film and television industry, working as a full union actor with the Union of British Columbia Performers (UBCP/ACTRA) from 2008 to 2018. My first theatre production in

"Celebrating Canada Day". 2016. *Taken on Lonsdale Ave., North Vancouver, B.C., Canada.*

Canada was "How the Other Half Loves" [2005/2006], and I was the first African American [black person] to perform on stage at the Bernie Legge Theatre in Queens Park, New Westminster. Proudly. New Westminster was once the capital city of B.C. and the Bernie Legge Theatre is one of its oldest venues. I'm honoured.

I met Dwayne, the lead actor in the play, and Chelsea, the director, and they helped me to shed my "American attitude and accent" and embrace my new surroundings in B.C. I enjoyed the production so much, I pursued more roles and a full-time career in performing arts.

Later, in 2007, I was cast in an outstanding, new work called "Quarterlife: The Musical," playing one of the lead roles, Julius, alongside a stellar group of five other performers. But I really knocked people's socks off when a lifetime dream came to fruition... In 2008, they cast me in "The Little Shop of Horrors" at Centennial Theatre in North Vancouver, as the voice of Audrey II. And then it snowed very hard. The highways and local roads were closed, but the show went on and the ensemble put on a stupendous performance. For those who attended, it was a show to remember.

In 2007, I had written a song about this leg of my journey titled "*Smile Every Now and Then.*" In 2009, someone asked me to perform it with an all-star live band Shawn Soucy, Brian, Eric, and Bill Sample at the 9th Annual World Kindness Concert in Vancouver, British Columbia, sponsored in part by Kindness Rocks and Brock Tully. "*Smile Every Now and Then*" became my anthem, my mantra, my way of life: Smile when you feel like smiling...remember to reserve moments in life to simply be happy.

Since the theatre scene in Vancouver did not have many options for me, I turned my attention to the television and film industry. After securing a few commercials and movie and TV roles, I worked as an actor. Three years later, I joined the union and continued working as a full member of the Union of British Columbia Performers (UBCP) and ACTRA. I also performed on stage as a vocalist, collaborated with artists on albums, and did studio work for both music and radio.

Aaron Turner, Jr.

8:3 Ask An Expert, Aaron - the original internet Avatar. Turner, Jr. A.
Ask An Expert, Aaron. *n.d. Screenshot image. Futureshop, internet*
avatar, 2008-2012.

I was also the first Internet Avatar in Canada as the "Ask an Expert" on the Future Shop website for a few years. I worked on the movie "Andromeda Strain," playing Private Connors, and appeared in a few short films, including a special work called "Ashes Fall." I voiced many radio jingles and advertisements; me, a singer with a hole in his throat.

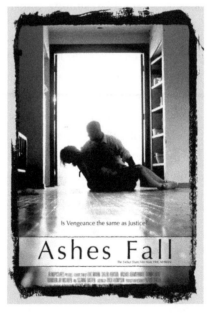

"the Ashes Fall film was a masterpiece!" I had the pleasure of filming
this amazing short with writer/director Eric Maran[Ashes Fall], in
2008. He chose this image as the poster art; courtesy of Blind Pictures.

My career in Vancouver was on the rise. I was still healing through the arts, and I only felt physical pain when I was in between shows. I stayed very active. To stay balanced, and because we had moved to Vancouver to enjoy the great outdoors, it's time to tell that story... of how Love Heals All Wounds, naturally.

BE SURE TO VISIT **WWW.IFYOUBELIEVE.ONLINE** TO SEE, HEAR, and experience the Chronicles of Aaron Junior Turner.

Act 8
IF YOU BELIEVE IN... LOVE

I t was 2003. I met my wife and the love of my life, Jennifer, through a friend, in a karaoke bar in the middle of San Francisco. Jenn was the program director of the Public Utilities Commission Early Childhood Education campus for the State of California and had just switched into the family childcare field. She was friends with the bar owners, knew all the staff, and was popular there. I found out later she went there because it wasn't a "meat market." Jen was an introvert—she just wanted a place to enjoy music, friends, and life in between working, going camping, and creating her art. She is an abstract artist who works in mixed media, as well as a children's book illustrator. I, on the other hand, am an extrovert.

I was making a new life for myself in San Francisco, focusing on sound design. I got an apartment six long San Francisco blocks away from the karaoke bar—and it had a stage where I could sing. The first time I met Jen, we talked for hours; we sat up in the bar throughout the night. I found out that she'd grown up in Wolf Creek, Oregon, and had moved to San Francisco in her early teens. She had fond memories of growing up with wildlife and living deep in nature. I got that—I loved nature too, and I felt her connection to it.

Our romance moved quickly and in a short time, we found ourselves surrounded by the intoxication of love. I took her back to that same bar less than a year later to propose on stage. She said YES! And it feels like we haven't left each other's side since.

While planning our honeymoon in 2004, we were seeking serenity in a place less travelled. We weren't interested in the usual getaways, like the Bahamas, Hawaii, Jamaica, and so on, because it wasn't realistic that we'd ever live there. Instead, we wanted to experience a place we could feel comfortable enough to someday, maybe, call home. We wanted to enjoy ourselves on our first and only "homeymoon"!

"Children of Arbutus". 2003. Taken at Lake Berryessa, California.

IN OCTOBER 2004 WE "GOOGLED" (WHICH WAS *SEARCH.COM* AT the time) "the best places to live on earth." That was too broad. So, we sub-searched: "...and to work," or "...best education," or "...

entertainment and activities," and so on. We micro-searched cultures from around the world, and at other times, we narrowed our search based on demographics. We filtered the results as best we could in 2004, and were getting the same results.

While continuing our search in countries as far away as Germany and Switzerland (those two countries were often #1 and #2), we found that Munich and Zurich were often on the lists of "best places to live on earth." Vancouver, British Columbia, kept ranking third or fourth best and was always in the top ten places to live on the entire planet. (From 2004 to the present, it has continued to rank high on these same lists.)

Our criteria included: lots of nature, lots of water, more trees than people, and slim to no war-mongering (outside of inner-quarrels). Our areas of interest were friendliness, diversity, and acceptance. Our goals were specific: We wanted to be adventurous and to explore outdoor living religiously! The more we researched, the more it seemed like we had discovered a hidden paradise in North America: Indigenous wilderness, untainted water, culture, winters I'd never experienced, and that Jen hadn't experienced since childhood.

Could Canada be the new destination for a pair of Northern California newlyweds who loved nature, peace, love (and now, poutine)? British Columbia is only about 1,000 miles away from the San Francisco Bay Area in California. We could drive to visit friends and family several times a year... and invite them to do the same. We could go hiking, whale-watching, and wake boarding all in the same week, and in some seasons, all on the same day. There was also a bustling city to enjoy and world-class seafood at any local market.

We became determined to explore B.C. (and to embrace all of Canada). We booked our tickets for a Homey-Moon in Vancouver. In December 2004, we took the Amtrak Train from San Francisco for a ten-day honeymoon in Vancouver. We'd previously purchased a

"Fodor's Canada travel guide," a "Vancouver Rough Guide," and a "Lonely Planet British Columbia & the Canadian Rockies" and used internet data to set a course. We travelled by bus and train for a day through a breathtaking wonderland in the snow-laden landscape of the Cascade mountains. It was gorgeous and romantic. We'd picked the perfect winter to travel.

"Homey-moon" 2004. Taken outside of the Vancouver Aquarium, B.C., Canada. We were on our honeymoon with Spinnaker, a Pacific White-Sided Dolphin, a beautiful Beluga whale, and we also adopted "HOPE"[J-Pod], a new-born Orca through the Orca/Killer Whale Adoption program.

We stayed in a high-rise in the heart of Vancouver: a time-share aptly named "the Canadian by Worldmark." The ground was covered in snow and the faces of the crowds were full of holiday cheer because it was December... St. Nick must have been nearby. Literally. This was the closest to the North Pole we had ever been. It was easy to celebrate love and melt into the holiday crowds. We knew that someday, absolutely, we would live here.

"Homeymooning on the B.C. Ferry". *January, 2004.*

WE TOOK OUR FIRST BC FERRY RIDE FROM TSAWWASSEN TO THE
Swartz Bay terminal on Vancouver Island. We continued by bus to
Victoria, B.C.'s capital city. It was a breathtaking and awe-inspiring
ferry ride through the islands. It took about ninety minutes, one-way.
It was our first time experiencing a large boat filled with cars and
passengers weaving in and out of small islands. The never-before-
seen blues, greens, and greys of the northern Pacific Ocean—so
beautiful. There were destination dream homes built on water's
edges of smaller islands between the larger islands. Pacific white-
sided dolphins splashed alongside the ferry, and there were sightings
of orca whales ahead. We felt like we were in the lost city of Atlantis
and we hadn't even reached shore yet. We had chosen the perfect
place to spend our honeymoon.

Coastline: the Gulf Islands, B.C. 2004. We are en route to Victoria, while admiring the red trees along the shore.

We were cuddling out on the ice-cold deck—experiencing a bone-chilling cold that was then new to us—both staring out at the island scenery: the granite... the greens... the reds, browns, and greys above the pristine water. There were hundreds of broad-leafed trees with distinctive red trunks and branches dotting the landscape. Jennifer called out, pointing to the shore, "Oh look, I grew up with those trees—Madrones. I miss them!"

"Madrona, the Madrone". 2011. A photo of the peeling skin on a Madrone tree, along the Oregon coast.

I looked in the direction she was pointing and replied, "You mean that bushel of over-sized Manzanitas?"

"No, those are Madrone trees," she insisted, "We have them all over Oregon...

I literally grew up with them by my side."

"Manzanito, the Manzanita bush". A 2004 photo of a tree from the Napa Valley area of Northern California.

I chuckled, "Those are Manzanitas, I'm certain of it. I can tell by the peeling skin.

I grew up with them, literally, outside my window."

In unison, we both said, "That's my favorite tree!"

...Which led to "No way!?" and "How cool!" ... and hugs and kisses.

But there was a conundrum—were they Manzanitas or Madrones? I turned to the on-deck attendant and asked, "Do you know the name of those trees?" He answered, "Oh, I sure do. Those are arbutus trees —local to the coastline. They're common... you'll see more farther up the way."

When we got to shore, we researched it further... it was true. They were arbutus trees... and they were everywhere! We were in Paradise. Within seconds of discovering this possible "parent" tree to the Manzanita and Madrone, we were in tears: it was a homey-moon to remember.

I realized later that those graceful, twisting trees, with their red flaking bark, drew us to our new life... in Canada... a place we have now called home for almost twenty years. When we realized that the Madrone and the Manzanita trees were now the children of the Arbutus tree, our collaboration, the "Children of Arbutus" was born. "COA," as we like to refer to our lifestyle, is travel, outdoor adventure, wildlife and water play. We write reviews of places we love, and we share them with the world. We document nature in photo, video, and song/lyric, and as the Children of Arbutus, we have accepted our place on Earth fully.

"Arby, the mighty Arbutus tree". 2013. Photograph. Sunshine Coast of British Columbia, Canada.

THE PEOPLE, THE PLACES, AND THE THINGS WE EXPERIENCED IN only ten days left us longing for more. How many totem poles could we experience in a lifetime? When could we explore the Kootenay Mountains or the Yukon Territories? While travelling through the train, airport, and ferry terminals, we often browsed the tourism fliers and brochures, and found we were sincerely interested in zip lining, crossing suspension bridges, hiking, and crabbing. There's the spectacular Sea-to-Sky Highway; in the Salish Sea, Killer Whales

Aaron Turner, Jr.

swim alongside ocean kayakers; and there are black bears in people's backyards in North and West Vancouver—usually, they are scared off with a "Boo!."

B.C. is beautiful!

Vancouver is also a multi-cultural melting pot of people—and a gorgeous city by the bay, a lot like San Francisco and other California coastal cities, such as San Diego and Monterey. For us two honeymooners, it was enchanting. B.C. felt like... well, home. It felt like (and was so similar to) some of our favourite aspects of Northern California: namely it has big, green trees and bright blue oceans. There are so many gorgeous places immediately accessible ... even on an injured foot. If you love nature—you'll love B.C. It's all God in the woods, you know.

OUR HOMEY-MOON WAS OVER TOO SOON. IN JANUARY 2005, WE travelled by train back to San Francisco. For twenty of the next twenty-seven hours, give or take, we brainstormed an exodus from our forever-so-beloved birthplaces, and from our home and sovereign country of California, into an unknown... a place we'd only ever heard referred to as "the Great White North."

Just six months later, we rented a twenty-four-foot U-Haul truck, hitched our VW Jetta to the back, waved goodbye to San Francisco, and set out to begin a new-life journey in B.C. We'd completed all the tests, screenings, and paperwork and had been approved to enter Canada for three years, or until they granted us citizenship.

"Totem-ly Cool!" 2004. A beautiful hand-carved Totem in Stanley Park, Vancouver, B.C., totally admired during our homeymoon vacation.

When we arrived, it felt like a celebration was scheduled on our behalf—a welcome party! Fireworks, we swear it. Decorations, parades! We had arrived on July 1st, 2005—Canada Day!

We were so happy that day. We'll never forget it. We arrived at the border and, by reading the weekly Metro Vancouver newspaper, "Learn everything you've ever wanted to know about Canada... Day," we learned just about everything we wanted to know. Canadians from Tofino to P.E.I. were celebrating and every person we spoke to was more than happy to express his or her love, pride, and adoration for all that stands behind the honorable Maple Leaf'd Red and White Canadian Flag.

Aaron Turner, Jr.

We knew we would build a glorious life here. We believed it from the moment we stepped off of the train during our homey-moon. We have always lived an amazing, adventure-filled life—as we have followed our dreams, scuttling around the Pacific Northwest... meeting people, sharing our experiences, writing music, creating art, and soaking in the best of people, places, and nature—Healing.

8.10. Three Identical Trees?

And that is the story of how we fell in love with beautiful, natural, Canada. We fell in love with nature; naturally—from the Golden Gate to the Lions Gate and everything in between. And now, after becoming acclimatized to life within a stone's throw of the magnificent Salish Sea, we are washed clean of old emotional patterns, and refreshed as "Two Crabs-One Shell", living our astrological dreams!. My love story with Jen, "Two Crabs-One Shell", is an accompanying blog, and was also the name we chose for our wedding theme in 2004. It has since grown into an online business and new chapter in our lives. It's a perfect name for us, as you'll discover if you visit our website and read our love story...with the moon: www.twocrabsoneshell.com.

Act 9
IF YOU BELIEVE IN... HUMANITY

It's 2020! The Vancouver skyline is the backdrop. I'm recording vocals in my at-home studio; "Anything Is Possible"[if you believe], the walls are covered with reviews of shows I've closed and there are some covers of albums I've been featured on or shows I've performed in. There are also announcements of the fitness workshops I've planned...but have been canceled due to the pandemic. To maintain my health, and to keep my rehabilitated body (and my mangled foot) in top form, I've become serious about keeping fit, and I've shared this passion with others through online workshops and coaching (more on that later). My life is designed with fitness in mind, and I carry the music with me; they work hand-in-hand.

After Dr. Bodner's surgery in 2000, I nursed my foot to the best of my ability. I learned about pro-inflammatory foods that caused pain and swelling in my feet and toes—and I learned to avoid them all, including red meat. During that fifteen-year stretch of learning to walk (and hike!) again, I realized that the more "I did," the faster I healed. The more active I became, the less I was in pain. The more I tried to do things, the less I had to try to do things.

Feed Me!. *Jan. 2009. Photo taken during rehearsal of Little Shop
Of Horrors [Audrey II), at Centennial Theater in North
Vancouver, B.C. Staged by Uncle Randy Productions.*

So, I decided to entertain more. I performed more often. I took
more courses, earned more credentials. I learned to stretch more,
and I ate even healthier. Even with applying all the knowledge of a
chef turned-performer turned-personal trainer, my foot still relapsed
in 2016. I was in pain again. That same year, I went back into surgery
with Dr. Alan K. Baggoo in North Vancouver, and he performed a
series of surgeries to "straighten" things out. Literally. I was suffering
from hammer toes and deformity. It was becoming impossible to
walk, so the doctor and his team severed the ligaments / muscles /
tendons in four of five toes and straightened them with screws. It
took six weeks for the recovery. With dedication and faith in your
ability to heal, even the impossible becomes possible. I frolic around
like a reindeer, sometimes, thanks to all the combined work of my
doctors. I never stopped believing I would heal.

I LOVE LIVING IN B.C. MY MARRIAGE IS WONDERFUL. JEN AND I have explored "Beautiful B.C." endlessly. We've become "real Canadians" ...Cascadian to say the least. We sometimes even pronounce "Zee" as "Zed," say "eh" at the ends of sentences and say "Sorry" even when an apology isn't called for. We also did that in California. We can both now name animals indigenous to our region on sight. We've seen moose, bears, coyotes, marmots, snakes, deer, porpoises, and dolphins in the wild. We're surrounded by bald eagles in a land where the caribou run wild and anyone can adopt an orca... symbolically. Healing.

We've acclimated to the grey B.C. rainforest weather (we both sense a tingle in our toes at the hint of foul weather). We've familiarized ourselves with B.C.'s culture(s), and, to the best of our abilities, we have assimilated to the regional customs. We've spoken intimately with youth and leaders of the Coast Salish, Similkameen, and other First Nations, and clearly, we still have a lot of exploring to do.

We are Canadian Citizens now. We were sworn in back in October 2017. Not much has changed since then. We've always felt a little Canadian and a little American, but North American all the same. We are grateful.

AS I FINISH WRITING THIS, WE ARE WELL INTO THE COVID-19 lockdown of 2020...2021. We have not yet tried the famous Quebecois treat, poutine—French-fried potatoes with thick gravy and cheese curds. We made a pledge, though—happily, poutine isn't just a Quebecers' delicacy anymore—and there's a poutine purveyor just a few blocks away—soon I'll be able to cross poutine off my "bucket list."

And speaking of a "bucket list," there's so much I still want to do in my life. A few years ago, I felt restless because I hadn't yet achieved everything I know I'm capable of. So, I began a business venture that would leverage my existing passion and my skills in the performing arts and combine them with fitness and nutrition, and culinary knowledge of yesteryear. I spent two years building the philosophy and program for a new venture: "AJ's Performing Arts Fitness." Often abbreviated as AJ's PAFITT because I follow the F.I.T.T. principals of exercise: frequency, intensity, time, and type. Cumulative results from the mind, body, and soul work I've mastered since that disastrous morning in 1998 on Atherton Avenue in Novato, California. PAFITT's signature program is "The Morning Motivation© ." (MOMO) I had been gearing up since my November 2019 startup; I only wanted to build from scratch. I did. I was about to have my launch in the community, including a grand opening public event scheduled for April 2020. Then, in mid-March, the pandemic was declared and the lockdown began. I had to pivot the business completely because they shut gyms and group fitness down. Fitness was still necessary, however, so I continued to support the clients who believed in my coaching.

AJ's Performing Arts Fitness, Logo. est. 2019.

People live in small homes—and small spaces—now. Big gyms are no longer easily accessible, like they were pre-pandemic. So, meal-planning and nutrition have moved to the forefront of my life. "A.J.'s Performing Arts Fitness" makes sense! If I can do it, so can you! I burn calories, while singing, in my small home gym. This will be my lifestyle for the foreseeable future. I don't know when I'll return to stage, and I've come so far to get back to it. Even when the pandemic ends, I doubt I will return to acting; but I will always stay fit. During the pandemic year of 2020 I created a crossword puzzle for my clients that reflects my coaching and beliefs in performing arts-style fitness training. I believe you can solve the puzzle at the end of the book; it starts with you now, and ends with you new. Good luck!

AaJuTu Music and Entertainment, Logo. est. 2013

I am also the owner-operator of AaJuTu Music & Entertainment, established in 2013. I work the most with Michael Nowak, the owner and sound engineer of Saga Recording Studio. He knows my voice well and I've done demo work and background vocals for others' albums. After a song is successful, we replace my voice with the principal vocalist's rendition; the song is released, and so on. I did this with other studios, and with artists in Santa Rosa and San Francisco... such is the world of a demo artist. It is always a pleasure and always a blessing to sing. Michael, in particular, works with fantastic artists and I enjoy being in his studio. I'll be working with him for years to come. He is a wonderful person and a master of his trade.

DURING THE 2020-2021 PANDEMIC RESTRICTIONS, I HONED MY performance and musical skills, building a studio with green screen and recording equipment, and learning new skills for self, and spiritual growth. I made the switch, like many others, in hopes to make myself available online. In the true fashion of a sensitive empath, I found time to entertain and uplift the world with some music and words of inspiration—and maintain private fitness sessions via Zoom. I released a new song called "Yesterday's Promises" on my Facebook page and launched a barebones version of my website: *www.myradiostation.ca*, dedicated to belief. I'm committed to spreading love and hope to those in need.

I've also been working on a song series, from hip hop to opera—all of the original music written and performed by myself over the past 25 years. I get a lot of help from my friend and musical genius, Mark Olexson. He co-wrote and helped produce "Let It All Go" and

www.myradiostation.ca, Logo. est. 2008

"Anything Is Possible" in 2013, and my debut song underscores the series. We make beautiful music, he and I—I look forward to sharing more of it.

WHETHER I CONTINUE MY CAREER AS A PERFORMING ARTIST remains to be seen—we all await what unfolds after the pandemic is over. But I know I'll always use my voice. I'll always put love first. I'll always take care of my health... and I believe in passing on that knowledge to whomever will listen. And soon, I'll have my next phase... on the brand-new, magical stage of the world... may God grant me the strength to do so.

Lately, I've been studying evidential mediumship and remote healing. Jennifer is a certified Moonologer and recently opened her online practice; Two Crabs-One Shell. Jennifer and I have both had experiences with angels. I'll be honest, I never believed I could speak to spirits, but I've always believed in guardian angels. I know I have one on my shoulder—and that's for sure! Left shoulder, to be exact.

I've emerged from my life experiences as a more enlightened individual, and I know I can face anything and persevere. Through my artistic creations I hope to help everyone see that life is a beautiful experience with endless possibilities, and that you can heal and come back from any tragedy. Twenty-plus years after my accident, I have a healing voice, a touching story, and an inspiring message: *Don't give up! Don't lose hope!*

Each of us experiences the same universal truths. We celebrate good times and we suffer bad times. I want to uplift, empower, and motivate others with my music and my memoir, as a reminder to others that...

ANYTHING IS POSSIBLE.

Just believe.

This photo was taken on or around April 26, 2013, during a visit to the traumatized tree and the owners, as well as Jim and Kathy Simontacci next door.

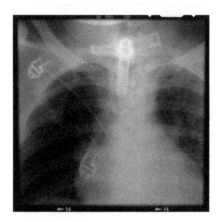

Please visit **www.ifyoubelieve.online** to hear the latest recording of the original song, "Anything Is Possible (If You Believe)", written and produced by Aaron J Turner and Mark Olexson, recorded at Saga Recording in Vancouver, BC, July 2013. AaJuTu Music.

JUST BELIEVE!

Please visit the website www.ifyoubelieve.online for a detailed list of images in this collage. Thank you.

EPILOGUE
A FINAL NOTE ON MY BELIEF IN HUMANITY

This story has been about my belief that anything is possible. But there's another story that needs to be told—my story about my life as a black man. I chose not to tell that story at the same time as my survival story. Why? Because it might have made you wonder why I still believe in humanity.

As I write this in 2021, the black lives matter movement is gaining strength, we are at the brink of world war three, and there are urgent events that need discussion. But not here and not now. Taking into consideration all that I've learned in forty-plus waking years thinking about being black, I feel lucky. I'm lucky to be alive in this skin, and happy to be walking around in it. Yes, I've experienced racism, and discrimination, and harassment, and you may have seen hints of that in the story you have just read. I may speak of that another day, but I do not believe in racism—and this book is about belief.

For now, I choose to believe that solutions will be found, and that one day, people of all colors, all backgrounds, all cultures, and all races will live together in 3-part, 4-part, and 7-part harmony.

PHOTOS & ILLUSTRATIONS

Heading/Epilogue. Gate,Alexander. *Through the heart.* April 23, 2021. Graphic art design. mystikmask.com.

Cover. Gate, Alexander. *Through the heart.* April 23, 2021. Graphic art design. mystikmask.com.

Back-Cover Photo. Jeff Craigen Photography, 2017

Cover Design. Gate, Alexander & Consalvo, Jennifer

Title. Turner, Jr. A. *AaJuTu Music and Entertainment Logo.* July, 2013. Graphic art design.

Unknown. *Glo-Jean; My Mother, My Queen High School Grad.* n.d. Photograph. Edited by Turner, Jr. A.

Consalvo, J. *Hugs and Voices...with his mother, embracing.* June 20, 2010. Hilltop Apostolic Church, Lower Lake, Ca.

Pre-Face. Unknown. *2010 Visiting my childhood home and surroundings,* California.

Acknowledgments. Healey, James. *Instruments Of Change.* Feb 5, 2015. Photograph. Live at the Imperial, Vancouver.

Introduction. Gate, Alexander. *Through the heart.* April 23, 2021. Graphic art design. mystikmask.com.

Heading. **Act** *1.1.* Turner, Jr. A. *A hole where my voice used to be.* June 14, 1998. Photograph. The tracheotomy removed after 6 weeks.

1.2 [FULL] Turner, Jr. A. *The Big Beach. Summer, 2010.* 2010. Photograph. Hidden Valley Lake at the big beach.

Heading. **Act** 2.1. Unknown. *Siblings-R-Us.* n.d. Photograph. With my older sister, Letitia, at age 2 and 4.

2.4. The Independent. *A Key To Heaven's Gate.* Monday, May 3, 1965. Photograph. News Article, reads "...hands the keys to the pastor of the new home of Bethel Temple Pentecostal Church [Richmond, California]...Accepting the new ownership ...from left, elder Joseph Turner, who founded the church in 1954; Jace Tanner, deacon, and Clinton N. Hendricks, secretary...".

Heading. **Act** *3.1.* Turner, Gloria. *I Be 3.* July 14, 1980. Photograph. Me, at the age of three.

3.5 and 3.6. Amador, Douglas. "Butterfingers belies his nickname just in time". Press Democrat; Empire Football, October 23, 1994.

3.7. Turner, Jr. A. *Jet Awake.* April 23, 1995. Photograph. Vehicle accident, 1987 VW JETTA after falling asleep at the wheel.

3.8 [Photo Collage] "Purple Reign", 1 high school graduation photo 2 high school graduation ceremony 3 high school football team photo.

Heading. **Act** 4.1. *Toe/Foot* Xray, Lions Gate Hospital Imagery. *Alright Stop! Hammertoes!.* Jan 2017. Photograph. Designed by Turner, Jr. A. Successful toe-straightening surgery by Dr. A. Baggoo to relieve pain and increase motion.

4.3. and 4.4. Tiffani Z. *Pleasure Point Hits The Proverbial G-Spot.* 1996. Photograph. Performing in the quad at SRJC under the then band name *Pleasure Point;* [left to right] Jonathan J., Jr., Andre W., Jr., Aaron T., Jr. , David C., article/review written by Arielle Kohn.

Heading. **Act** 5.1. Xray, Marine General Hospital Imagery. *Fix the Fib First, and the Feet will Follow!.* May, 1998. Photograph. Designed by Turner, Jr. A. The beginning of a series of lower-extremity, reconstructive surgeries, lasting several years.

5.6. Ground, Jeanie, "In loving memory of Aaron Turner—April 27, 1998", photo taken in April 1999.

5.8. White, S.E., Novato Community Hospital Imagery. *Profile 2.0.* 2015. Still Photograph, not used for production,. (on the left), taken on the set of "No Tomorrow", filmed in Vancouver, BC., and an Xray image taken May 1998, showing reconstructive surgery to mandible, jaw bone, sinus structure and nose, repaired using wires, pins, screws and skills.

[FULL] Turner, Jr. A. *Then To Now.* 2021. Photo Collage (a) youth photo at 16, Dawson Studios, (b) crushed face Xray from the morning of the accident (c) 6.5 weeks later (d) Film/TV headshot 2018...20 Years later, courtesy of Jeff Craigen Photography.

Heading. **Act** *6.1. u*nknown. May, 2003. Photograph. Graduation, Sonoma State University.

6.2. Turner, Jr. A. My Ticket to Ride. Jan 29, 1999. Photograph, Standup Tragedy at Santa Rosa Junior College theatre department.

6.4. Turner, Jr. A. *American College Theater Festival,* (a) *Award for Original Music Composition, Watermelon Nights by Greg Sarris.* Feb, 2000 (b) *Sound Design Finalist, Watermelon Nights.* Feb. 2000 (c) *Kate Drain Lawson Award, Sound Design, Halfway Diner b J. Sayles,* Feb. 2001 (d) *Regional Sound Design Winner, Halfway Diner.* Feb. 2001. Photocopy. *www.kennedy-center.org.*

6.6. Unknown/Sonoma State University School photographer. *A Magical moment in my life.* 2001. Photograph. In costume at the Sonoma State University production of the Opera/Musical Theatre piece,"the Magic Flute", by Mozart, directed by A. McTigue and with Musical direction from L. Morrow., promotional photograph.

6.9. Chown, Thomas. *Halfway Diner.* 2001. SRJC. Turner, Jr. A. singing original song, "Halfway Blues, Halfway Home"

[Full] unknown 2008 photo taken during the run of Quarterlife, musical, by Chantal Forde and Neville Bowman, Fiesty Fairy Productions, **winner of best new work at the Ovation Awards in Vancouver, B.C.

Heading. **Act** 7.1. Turner, Jr. A. *The Comedy and Tragedy of 2005.* 2005. Photograph. Mural/wall art on a building that no longer stands, Burnaby, B.C.

7.5 unknown "A magical moment in my life". 2001. *Mozart's opera blends the ridiculous and the sublime.* Press Democrat Newspaper.

Heading. **Act** 8.1. Turner, Jr. A./Consalvo, J. *Children of Arbutus.* 2003. Photograph. Taken while camping and boating at Lake Berryessa, California.

Heading. **Act** 9.1. Fierro, Ron. *Live at Library Square, Vancouver, B.C.* 2011. Photograph. Turner, Jr. A. singing with the Soul Assembly Band. Photo by Ron Fierro Photography.

Xray. Tracheotomy. Novato Community Hospital Imagery. *A Hole In My Throat.* April 1998/May1998. Photograph. Designed by Turner, Jr. A.

**AJ's Performing Arts Fitness Crossword Puzzle, 2020, designed by A. Turner, Jr., owner, @PAFITT, marketing and client research.

BIBLIOGRAPHY

BOOKS AND PRINT PUBLICATIONS:

Ayckbourn, Alan. *How the Other Half Loves*. New York: Samuel French Inc., 1971. Print.

Benson, Bernard S. *The Peace Book*. New York: Peace Child International, 1982. Print.

Cain, Bill. *Stand Up Tragedy*. New York City: Samuel French, 1991. Print.

Crichton, Michael. *The Andromeda Strain*. New York: A.A. Knopf, 1969. Print.

Edgar, David. *Continental Divide: Daughters of the Revolution and Mother's Against*. London: Nick Hern Books Limited, 2004. Print.

Fodor's. *Fodor's Canada, 27th Edition (Travel Guide)*. Los Angeles: Fodor's, 2004. Print.

Forde, Chantelle. *Quarterlife: The Musical.* Vancouver: Feisty Fairy Productions, 2007. Print.

Jepson, Tim. *Vancouver.* New York: Rough Guides, 2004. Print.

Menken, Alan and Howard Ashman. *Little Shop of Horrors.* North Vancouver: Uncle Randy Productions, 2009. Print.

Mozart, Wolfgang Amadeus. *the Magic Flute: An Opera in Two Acts.* New York: G. Schirmer, 1941. Print.

O'Neill, Eugene. *Anna Christie.* New York: Dover Publications, 1998. Print.

Saris, Greg. *Watermelon Nights.* New York: Hyperion, 1998. Print.

Ver Berkmoes, Ryan and Graham Neale. *British Columbia.* Footscray: Lonely Planet Publications., 2004. Print.

Wasserman, Dale. *Beggar's Holiday.* Mill Valley: Marin Theatre Company, 2004. Print.

Woollcombe, David and Rosy Simonds. *Peace Child.* Cambridge: Peace Child International, 1982. Print.

CREDITS & APPEARANCES

PLAYS: MY CREDITS

Anna Christie, written by Eugene O'Neill, Dir. Lee D. Sankowich, Dean Lester Regional Centre for the Arts, Walnut Creek, CA, March 25, 2004.

https://www.abouttheartists.com/productions/124062-anna-christie-at-dean-lesher-regional-center-for-the-arts-2004.

Beggar's Holiday, written by Dale Wasserman and John LaTouche, Dir. Lee D. Sankowich, Marin Theatre Company Boyer Theatre, Mill Valley, CA, September 9, 2004.

https://en.wikipedia.org/wiki/Beggar%27s_Holiday.

https://www.sfgate.com/bayarea/article/Embracing-a-new-stage-in-life-Crash-victim-2693383.php.

https://www.abouttheartists.com/productions/28488-beggars-holiday-at-marin-theatre-company-boyer-theatre-september-9-october-10-2004.

Continental Divide, Mothers Against, Daughters of the Revolution, written by David Edgar, Dir. Tony Taccone, Berkeley Rep Roda Theatre, Berkeley CA, November 6, 2003 (Understudy, no appearances).

How the Other Half Loves, written by Alan Ayckbourn, Dir. Chelsea McPeake, Vagabond Players, Bernie Legge Theatre, New Westminster, B.C., Nov. 2, 2005.

https://www.vagabondplayers.ca/past-productions.

Little Shop of Horrors, written by Alan Mencken and Howard Ashman, Dir. Richard Berg,

Centennial Theatre, North Vancouver, B.C., January 6, 2009.

https://robert-sondergaard.com/little-shop-of-horrors.

https://reviewvancouver.org/th_little_shop09.htm.

Peace Child, written by David Woolcombe and Bernard S Benson, Music and lyrics by David Gordon, Peace Child Foundation, performed at schools in US 1984-1986.

https://peacechild.org/our-history/.

http://www.peacechildthemusical.com/primary-school-peace-child/.

Stand Up Tragedy, written by Bill Cain, Dir. Unknown, Luther Burbank Auditorium, Santa Rosa, CA, 1999.

https://theatrearts.santarosa.edu/archived-seasons.

Watermelon Nights, written by Greg Saris, Dir. Leslie McCauley, Luther Burbank Auditorium, Santa Rosa, CA, 1999.

https://theatrearts.santarosa.edu/archived-seasons.

Halfway Diner, written by John Sayles, Dir. Leslie McCauley, Luther Burbank Auditorium, Santa Rosa, CA, 2000.

https://theatrearts.santarosa.edu/archived-seasons.

MUSIC: MY CREDITS

Brock Tully. *The 9th Annual World Kindness Concert*. 2009. Vancouver Community College.

https://brocktully.com/kindness-central/.

AJ Turner, "Can't Be in Two Places," 1999. Performed live. www.myradiostation.ca.

AJ Turner, "Halfway Home, Halfway Blues," 2000. Performed live. www.myradiostation.ca

AJ Turner, "Smile Every Now and Then," 2007. AaJuTu Music & Entertainment. Digital. www.myradiostation.ca. And *The 9th Annual World Kindness Concert*. 2009. Vancouver Community College.

AJ Turner, "Yesterday's Promises," 2020. AaJuTu Music & Entertainment. Digital. www.myradiostation.ca.

AJ Turner "Anything Is Possible," 2013. AaJuTu Music & Entertainment. Digital.

www.myradiostation.ca.

AJ Turner "Let It All Go," 2015. AaJuTu Music & Entertainment. Digital. www.myradiostation.ca.

FILM: MY CREDITS

Maran, Eric, dir., writer. *Ashes Fall*. 2007; Blindpictures.

https://www.imdb.com/title/tt0980944/.

https://vimeo.com/157877127.

WEB: MY CREDITS

Future Shop/Ask an Expert. Canadian electronics store chain, 2008-2012.

Future Shop Community. *"Future Shop Meet Aaron and Fred."* Accessed 2021.

https://community.khoros.com/t5/Past-Lithys/Most-Innovative-Community-Future-Shop-Meet-Aaron-amp-Fred-The/idi-p/5736.

TV: MY CREDITS

The Andromeda Strain. 2008. TV 4-part Mini-Series. Directed by Mikael Salomon. Aired May 26, 2008.

https://www.imdb.com/title/tt0424600/.

My Book. "If You Believe: A Memoir To Inspire Healing"

MOVIES:

Allers, Roger, and Rob Minkoff. 1994. *The Lion King.* United States: Buena Vista Pictures.

https://en.wikipedia.org/wiki/The_Lion_King_(musical).

Spielberg, Steven, dir.1985. *The Color Purple.* United States: Warner Bros.

https://en.wikipedia.org/wiki/The_Color_Purple_(film).

Wachowski, Lana, and Lilly Wachowski, creators.1999. *The Matrix.* United States: Warner Bros.

https://en.wikipedia.org/wiki/Morpheus_(The_Matrix).

Zemeckis, Robert, dir. 1994. *Forrest Gump.* United States: Paramount Pictures.

https://en.wikipedia.org/wiki/Forrest_Gump.

PLAYS:

Begulein, Chad, writer. Menken, Alan, composer. Clements, Ron, and John Musker, producer, director. "Aladdin." [New York, NY]: Disney, 2014.

https://www.abouttheartists.com/productions/68917-disneys-aladdin-at-new-amsterdam-theatre-2014.

Manley, Jay. director. Monroe, James, actor. "Sweeney Todd: the Demon Barber of Fleet Street." [Los Altos Hills, California]: Foothill College, 2005.

https://foothill.edu/theatre/archives/todd/.

Miranda, Lin-Manuel, actor, writer, music. Ron Chernow, writer. "Hamilton: an American Musical." [New York City]: The Public Theatre, 2015.

https://en.wikipedia.org/wiki/Hamilton_(musical).

TV SHOWS:

Brown, Michael, Narrator. Rankin, Steven, producer. 2013. *Naked and Afraid*. June 23, 2013 to present. Discovery Channel.

https://en.wikipedia.org/wiki/Naked_and_Afraid.

Hyams, John, Dir. 2015. *Alone*. June 18, 2015 to present. History.

https://en.wikipedia.org/wiki/Alone_(TV_series).

Stroud, Les, Dir. 2005. *Survivorman*. April 6, 2005 – December 13, 2016. OLN.

https://en.wikipedia.org/wiki/Survivorman.

MUSIC: REFERENCED

Bette Midler, vocalist, "Wind Beneath My Wings," 1989, Side 1 Beaches Original Motion Picture Soundtrack, Atlantic Records, Vinyl 7," 45 RPM.

https://www.imdb.com/name/nm0000541/

Blackstreet. American R&B group. 1993-2003, 2014 to present.

https://en.wikipedia.org/wiki/Blackstreet.

Boyz II Men. American vocal harmony group. 1987 to present.

https://en.wikipedia.org/wiki/Boyz_II_Men.

David Gordon, "I Want To Live," 1982-1984, Track 7 *Peace Child the Musical*, Apocalypse Music, Peace Child Song Book.

https://www.peacechildthemusical.com/the-peace-child-song-book/.

David Gordon, "Mr. President," 1982-1984, Track 17. *Peace Child the Musical*, Apocalypse Music, Peace Child Song Book.

https://www.peacechildthemusical.com/the-peace-child-song-book/.

Jodeci. American R&B quartet. 1989 to present.

https://en.wikipedia.org/wiki/Jodeci.

Lemuel Turner, "Jake Bottle Blues," recorded February 9, 1928, Side B on *Traveler into the Blue*, Victor, Shellac 10," 78 RPM.

https://www.youtube.com/watch?v=LxeP3mJ3yS4.

Lemuel Turner, "Way Down Yonder Blues," recorded February 7, 1928, Side A, steel guitar solo, Victor, Shellac 10," 78 RPM.

https://www.youtube.com/watch?v=WoMFF5tLiL8.

Mahalia Jackson, "Walk with Me (Lord)," recorded 1964, Track B5 on *Sing Out,* Kenwood Records, Vinyl LP (reissue).

https://www.youtube.com/watch?v=ZfZItAoIgs4.

Mike and Peggy Seeger vocalists, "The Itsy-Bitsy Spider" ("The Eency-Weensy Spider"), 1948. Side 2 Track 5 on *American Folksongs for Children,* vinyl LP.

https://www.allmusic.com/album/american-folksongs-for-children-mw0000194780.

https://en.wikipedia.org/wiki/Itsy_Bitsy_Spider.

Shai. American Vocal R&B / Soul Quartet. 1991 to present.

https://en.wikipedia.org/wiki/Shai_(band).

Tom Glazer, "On Top of Spaghetti," recorded 1963, Do- Re- Mi Children's Chorus, Kapp Records, Vinyl LP.

https://www.youtube.com/watch?v=tSbSjRJ9xz4.

Winans, The. American Gospel Quartet. 1980 to present.

https://en.wikipedia.org/wiki/The_Winans.

THINGS:

Canadian by Worldmark, Vancouver, B.C. Timeshare. Accessed August 2021.

https://clubwyndham.wyndhamdestinations.com/us/en/resorts/wyndham-hotels-resorts/canada/british-columbia/vancouver/worldmark-vancouver-the-canadian.

Lacrosse, Little Brother of War/Choctaw Stickball. History of Lacrosse. Accessed August 2021.

https://en.wikipedia.org/wiki/History_of_lacrosse.

Nintendo Video Games. "Super Mario," Metroid, Tetris. 1983 to present. Accessed August 2021. https://en.wikipedia.org/wiki/Nintendo_video_game_consoles.

https://en.wikipedia.org/wiki/Super_Mario.

https://en.wikipedia.org/wiki/Metroid.

https://en.wikipedia.org/wiki/Tetris.

People:

Calloway, Sway and King Tech. "The Wake-Up Show." Host at 106.1 KMEL. American urban contemporary radio station. SF, CA. IHeartMedia. Accessed August 2021.

https://en.wikipedia.org/wiki/KMEL

da Vinci, Leonardo. Italian Renaissance artist. Accessed August 2021.

https://en.wikipedia.org/wiki/Leonardo_da_Vinci. Accessed August 2021.

Hendrix, Jimmy. American musician, singer, and songwriter. Accessed August 2021.

https://en.wikipedia.org/wiki/Jimi_Hendrix.

https://www.jimihendrix.com/

Jackson, Chris. American actor and composer. Accessed August 2021.

https://www.imdb.com/name/nm1862960/

Ming Trent, Jacob. Born Boston Massachusetts. American actor. Accessed August 2021.

https://www.imdb.com/name/nm2850805/

Newcombe, Brian. Session bassist. B.C., Canada. Accessed August 2021.

http://www.e-studio-bassplayer.com/.

https://www.discogs.com/artist/674040-Brian-Newcombe

Novak, Michael. Owner, Engineer. Saga Recording Studios. B.C., Canada. Accessed August 2021.

http://www.sagarecording.com/

Obama, Barack. 44th President of the United States. January 8, 1997 – November 4, 2004. Accessed August 2021.

https://en.wikipedia.org/wiki/Barack_Obama.

Olexson, Mark. Multi-instrumentalist, vocalist, performer, and producer. B.C., Canada. Accessed August 2021.

https://www.facebook.com/Mark-Olexson-99688740063/

Reed, Eric. Live performance and studio multi-instrumentalist. B.C., Canada. Accessed August 2021.

http://www.ericreed.org/themusician.htm.

Sample, Bill. Canadian composer, producer, arranger, and pianist. B.C., Canada. Accessed August 2021.

https://billsamplemusic.com/

Soucy, Shawn. Professional drummer and percussionist. B.C., Canada. Accessed August 2021.

https://www.instagram.com/drumsetc/.

https://m.facebook.com/ShawnSoucyDrumsetc/

Weeden, Derek Lee. Actor and writer. Oregon, USA. Accessed August 2021.

https://www.abouttheartists.com/artists/315555-derrick-lee-weeden.

https://www.imdb.com/name/nm2899365/

Turner, Aaron Junior. Actor, Singer, and Composer. California, USA. B.C., Canada (Self)

https://www.ifyoubelieve.online

https://www.imdb.com/name/nm2579382/

*cover and interior designed by A. Turner, Jr. and J. Consalvo, Two Crabs - One Shell

NOTES

1. IF YOU BELIEVE

1. See my song, "Smile Every Now and Then," inspired by my accident, at: https://www.facebook.com/128238983901019/videos/10150094675865119/.

4. IF YOU BELIEVE IN… FATE

1. See my website for more information, at www.myradiostation.ca

7. IF YOU BELIEVE IN… THE HEALING ARTS

1. AJ was featured in an article on his role in "Beggar's Holiday." https://www.sfgate.com/bayarea/article/Embracing-a-new-stage-in-life-Crash-victim-2693383.php.

Thank You

AJ's
PAFITT
PERFORMING ARTS FITNESS

DOWN

1 (3 Letters)
Who is the most important person at the beginning of your fitness goal?

2 (8 Letters)
Who can best help you safely, fast and effectively reach your fitness goals?

3 (4 Letters)
Exercises that are often performed on water, but can also be achieved in gyms.

6 (5 Letters)
Low-impact, treadmill-driven workouts, that burn calories and tone muscles, to improve your resting heart rate for optimal health.

7 (3 Letters)
A soft-engineered foam, used during fitness and yoga, to pad or prevent injury.

8 (7 Letters)
To refresh the body with energizing fluids and necessary electrolytes.

10 (9 Letters)
An upright, total-body workout machine, designed for optimal cardio-vascular health.

14 (2 Letters)
Trainers like myself are very intuitive and use Direct Communication, also referred to as Direct Current, to scan the physical body for hidden inhibitors; often abbreviated as _ _?

15 ((5 Letters)
Spinning in place on a ____ to improve your overall health - mimicking riding a bike outdoors.

17 (3 Letters)
Who's the best friend any friend could ever have?

ACROSS

3 (3 Letters)
To move faster than a walk, and slower than a sprint, but similar to a jog.

4 (3 Letters)
The place in time where you are today and the only place your body can be.

5 (4 Letters)
An exercise only performed in water.

8 (4 Letters)
A mobility exercise performed only in nature, on or off trail.

9 (5 Letters)
Seven-to-Nine hours of dezzzzzzignated time for cell recovery, restoration and brain health.

11 (4 Letters)
Having fun while performing or staying fit just for the heck of it.

12 (3 Letters)
How do you get energy in.

13 (4 Letters)
The most functional movements of the body are the hinge, the twist, a squat, lunges, push and _____ ?

14 (5 Letters)
A group exercise where you burn calories while moving your body to rhythmic music.

16 (4 letters)
Generally speaking, the diaphragm, or rectus abdominus muscles, internal and external obliques, and the larynx organ, together with pitch are necessary to _____ on stage.

18 (4 Letters)
At the end of workouts, be sure to ____ down.

19 (3 Letters)
The end result of replacing old habits.

20 (6 Letters)
A 2 to 5 minute routine, before your workout, involving static and/or dynamic stretching.

IT STARTS WITH YOU, *NOW* - IT ENDS WITH YOU, *NEW!*

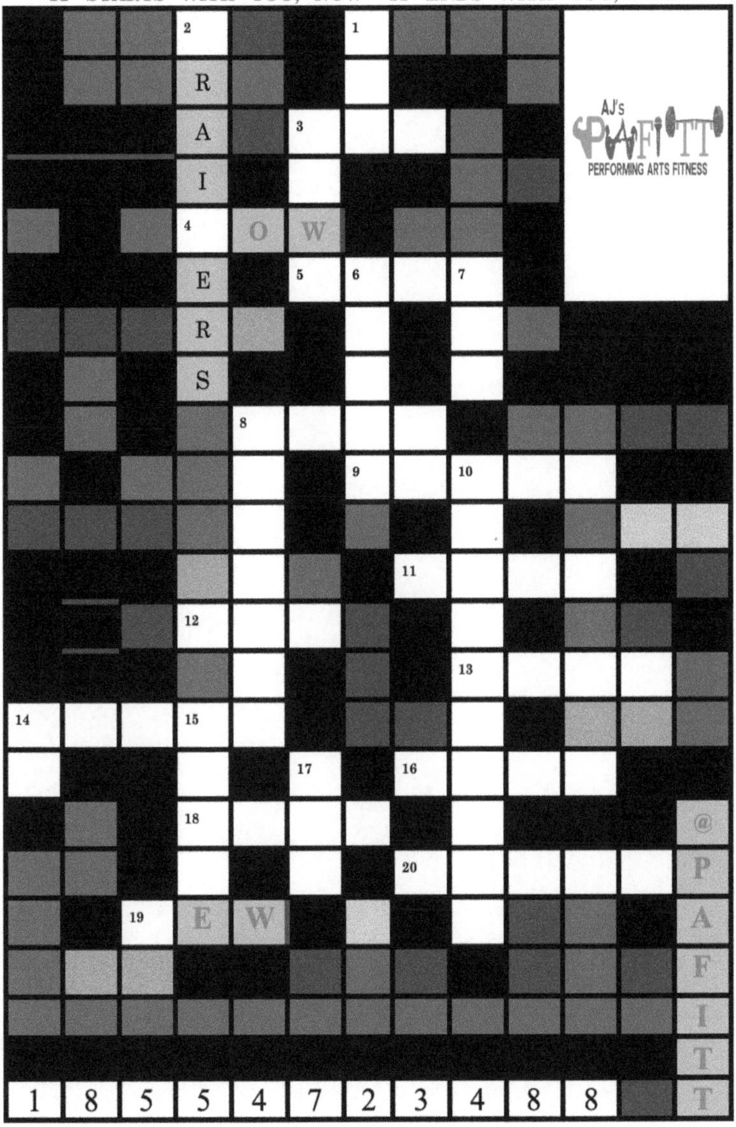
AJ's
PERFORMING ARTS FITNESS
R
A
I
O W
E
R
S
E W
@
P
A
F
I
T
T
1 8 5 5 4 7 2 3 4 8 8

CPSIA information can be obtained
at www.ICGtesting.com
Printed in the USA
BVHW011515010722
641098BV00010B/163

9 781777 909109